BARRON'S

HSPA

NEW JERSEY LANGUAGE ARTS LITERACY TEST

2ND EDITION

Edie Weinthal, Ph.D.
District English Supervisor
2007 New Jersey "Outstanding Language Arts Educator"
(New Jersey Council Teachers of English)
Pascack Valley Regional High School District
Montvale, NJ

Patricia Hade, M.A.
Former English Teacher
Pascack Valley Regional High School District
Montvale, NJ

BARRON'S

This book is dedicated to Dr. Barbara Sapienza—friend, colleague, mentor, and master educator—who led by example and inspired others by her faith in their abilities.

EW

Acknowledgments

Jennings Michael Burch, *They Cage the Animals at Night*. The Penguin Group: New York, 1984.

Jay Sommer, *Journey to the Golden Door: A Survivor's Tale*. Shengold Publishers, Inc.: New York, 1994.

UNEP Executive Director, "Message for World Water Day from UNET Information" NOTE 2002/6, 22 March 2002.

Animal Protection Institute, "Adopting a Companion Animal," "Home Aquariums," and "Breaking the No-Pet Rule."

All photographs courtesy of Sandra Weinthal, photographer (unless otherwise noted).

All inquiries should be addressed to:
Barron's Educational Series, Inc.
250 Wireless Boulevard
Hauppauge, New York 11788
www.barronseduc.com

Library of Congress Control Number: 2008018767

ISBN-13: 978-0-7641-4017-4
ISBN-10: 0-7641-4017-5

Library of Congress Cataloging-in Publication Data

Weinthal, Edie.
HSPA New Jersey language arts literacy / by Edie Weinthal, Patricia Hade.—2nd ed.
   p. cm.
Rev. ed. of: How to prepare for the New Jersey language arts literacy HSPA examination. 2003.
Includes index.
ISBN-13: 978-0-7641-4017-4
ISBN-10: 0-7641-4017-5
1. Language arts (Secondary)—New Jersey—Examinations, questions, etc.—Study guides.
2. High schools—New Jersey—Graduation requirements—Study guides. 3. Educational tests and measurements—New Jersey—Study guides. I. Hade, Patricia. II. Weinthal, Edie. How to prepare for the New Jersey language arts literacy HSPA examination. III. Title.

LB1631.5.W47 2008
428.1071'2—dc22   2008018767

Printed in the United States of America
9 8 7 6 5 4 3 2 1

Contents

Contents

Chapter 1	# The New Jersey HSPA in Language Arts Literacy

WHAT IS "HIGH-STAKES" TESTING AND HOW DOES IT AFFECT <u>YOU</u>?

You have been taking tests your entire school career: essay tests, workbook tests, vocabulary quizzes, short-answer tests, and multiple-choice tests, to name but a few. Some of you may have taken I.Q. tests, Terra Nova tests, Standford tests, or perhaps an entrance exam when you began high school. Many of these tests were ones for which you studied, whereas some tested aptitude or general knowledge, so there was no advance preparation.

The introduction of **high-stakes testing** is one part of the movement to create high standards in public schools. High-stakes tests **carry serious consequences for students and educators**. They lead to important decisions for students, such as tracking, special placements (gifted, special education), promotion, graduation, scholarship awards, and higher education admissions.

More than twenty-four states now require high school seniors to pass a test to get a diploma, and New Jersey is one of those states. Our test is called the High School Proficiency Assessment (HSPA, for short). This test will be given in your junior year of high school over a period of several days. To graduate from high school in New Jersey, it is necessary to pass this test. If you do not pass on the first try, you will have to attend classes or special learning programs to gain the skills needed to pass.

The HSPA is a high-stakes test, and it is important to do your best on it. A passing grade on the HSPA means, according to the Department of Education of New Jersey, that a student has acquired the knowledge and skills needed to graduate from a New Jersey high school. The next section of this book will explain the specifics of the HSPA in Language Arts Literacy.

OVERVIEW OF THE NEW JERSEY HSPA IN LANGUAGE ARTS LITERACY

Language Arts is a subject area composed of many different kinds of skills that you have been practicing since you started school: reading, writing, speaking, listening, and viewing. All of these skills aid in communicating, and they all engage you in thinking critically about the world.

The New Jersey High School Proficiency Assessment (HSPA, for short) in Language Arts Literacy is designed to test language arts skills. A passing grade will indicate that you have mastered the skills required to read critically and to communicate through writing in a clear and organized fashion.

The HSPA in Language Arts Literacy is a five-part test given over a two-day period. It consists of an assortment of tasks, including reading, writing, editing, and answering multiple-choice questions. Each of these tasks will be explained in detail in the rest of this book. For now, let's just look at what each part will ask you to do over the two days:

- **PART ONE**: Write an <u>extended response</u> to a given photograph.

- **PART TWO**: Read a <u>persuasive selection</u> and answer multiple-choice and <u>open-ended</u> questions about the text.
- **PART THREE**: Read a <u>narrative selection</u> and answer multiple-choice and open-ended questions about the text.
- **PART FOUR**: Write a <u>persuasive essay</u> or letter in response to a specific <u>prompt</u>.
- **PART FIVE**: Revise and edit text.

For an explanation of any of the underlined terms, see the "**Terms You Should Know**" section of this chapter.

HOW WILL MY TEST BE SCORED?

Like other standardized tests you have taken, your answer sheet for the HSPA will be sent away for scoring. The multiple-choice questions will be scored by machine, but the writing portions will be graded <u>holistically</u> by trained readers based upon a specific <u>rubric</u>. (Once again, check "**Terms You Should Know**" if you are unfamiliar with the meanings of underlined words.)

The Language Arts HSPA should not be a "scary" test to take. If you can read and write, you have the basic tools needed to do well on the Language Arts HSPA. You can help yourself by understanding what the test questions are asking, by becoming familiar with the format of the test, and by practicing reading passages and writing tasks that are similar to those that will be on the test. This book is designed to help you do these things.

TERMS YOU SHOULD KNOW

- **Prompt**: A writing prompt is the set of directions explaining exactly what the writing task is requiring you to do. Make sure to read the prompt <u>carefully and completely</u> because it contains important information and may ask you to do more than one thing in your writing. You want to be certain to respond to every part of the writing prompt.
- **Extended response**: This is a timed response that you must write as you answer a specific prompt. The two extended-response questions on the HSPA in Language Arts are the response to the picture and the persuasive essay or letter you will be asked to write. The extended-response questions will require you to write well-organized, multiple paragraphs that answer all parts of the writing task.
- **Persuasive selection**: To *persuade* is to convince someone of your point of view by using examples, facts and statistics, and logic. As you read the persuasive selection, take notice of the techniques used by the author to "sway" the reader. When asked to write your own persuasive extended response, try to use some of these same techniques to convince the reader of your ideas.
- **Open-ended questions**: Open-ended questions, which follow each reading selection and set of multiple-choice questions, ask you to *write* a response that will show you have understood the text. Whereas the multiple-choice questions ask you to select one of four possible answers to a given question, the open-ended questions ask you to *think* about what you have read, and to write one or more paragraphs that show insight into the reading selection. As you work through the examples we have given on open-ended questions, note that the open-ended questions consist of a number of specific ideas you are asked to address. You will have to make certain to answer each part of the open-ended question.
- **Narrative selection**: The *narrative* selection is one that "tells a story." It could be a short story, an essay, a description, or even a part of a long novel. *Narrate* means "to tell," and you will notice that the authors of the narrative selections aren't trying to per-

suade you to their point of view; rather, they have other reasons for relating their stories. Narration has many purposes, such as entertainment, explaining, describing, or making a specific point about something, to name a few.

- **Rubric**: A rubric is a chart with specific criteria (guidelines) to help readers score written responses. There are different rubrics for each of the different written responses on the HSPA. As a reader reads what you have written, he or she "compares" the written work with the specifics on the rubric for that writing task. Using the same set of standards, a rubric allows readers to compare your paper with someone else's for the most objective evaluation possible.

- **Holistic scoring**: *Holistic* means "whole," and this is the way that everything you *write* on the HSPA will be scored. (The multiple-choice questions will be scored in a different way.) Using a rubric, as described above, the person scoring your writing will look at the *whole* text and determine how well all of the elements in the writing work together to convey your ideas. You will receive a single *holistic* score for each written portion; the score takes into account each element of the rubric but is an overall evaluation of how successfully you have accomplished the writing task.

HOW TO USE THIS BOOK

This book is designed to help you practice for the New Jersey High School Proficiency Assessment in Language Arts Literacy. It is organized into seven chapters, including this introductory chapter. We believe that your chances of doing well on the HSPA will be greatly improved as you become familiar with the way the test will look and with the HSPA-required tasks.

Each of the following chapters addresses <u>one</u> of the HSPA tasks. In each of these chapters there is an overview, indicating the directions that will be given for each task and explaining what you are being asked to do. Next, the question is broken down into the step-by-step process needed to complete each task. We have tried to provide numerous strategies and helpful hints along the way. Each chapter will explain how each task will be scored and provide sample answers based on that scoring method. The chapters containing multiple-choice questions give correct answers and explain the skills needed to answer specific questions. In the "Putting It All Together" section at the end of each chapter, you will have an opportunity to practice the task that was the focus of the chapter.

Chapter 7 offers two full-length HSPA practice tests so that you can experience the entire test. Tests should be taken after practicing the individual tasks in the initial chapters.

As you work your way through this book, make certain to understand each task thoroughly before moving on. Do take the practice tests using the steps learned in each chapter, and do compare your responses with the ones provided.

Make sure to take plenty of study breaks, and don't try to absorb too much at one sitting. After you feel comfortable with a particular task, move on to the next chapter.

TEST PREPARATION

There are three "stages" of test preparation for the New Jersey HSPA in Language Arts Literacy. You have been involved in the first stage of test preparation since beginning school eight to ten years ago: reading and writing. As you engage in reading more and more types of textual materials (books, magazines, newspapers, dramas, journals, research materials, and fictional and nonfictional readings, to name a few), your ability to do well on the New Jersey HSPA in Language Arts Literacy improves. Reading strategies learned on your own or in school will help on the HSPA.

Engaging in frequent and different types of writing tasks (essays, short answers, paraphrasing, summaries, research papers, and argumentative, persuasive, and narrative papers) will also help with the New Jersey HSPA in Language Arts Literacy. Remember, the HSPA is designed to test the language arts skills acquired over the years.

As the date of the HSPA approaches, you are ready to begin the second stage of test preparation. A test prep book such as this one will help you understand the specific reading and writing tasks required for success on the New Jersey HSPA in Language Arts Literacy. Begin reviewing early enough to have time to understand each chapter and to attempt practice tests for each task. Make certain to complete at least one "real" HSPA in Language Arts Literacy from start to finish to get the full test experience before the actual test date.

The third stage of test preparation comes the weekend or night before the test. Do not try to cram information at this stage! Rather, be calm and confident because you practiced during "stage two." Now is the time to take the night or weekend off—but try to get plenty of rest!

Make certain to eat a good breakfast on the morning of the HSPA, so that your stomach isn't growling halfway through the test. Remember to bring several sharpened pencils, a watch, perhaps some water, and a quick snack if you think you will need it. Wear something comfortable, because you will be sitting for a long period of time. To do your best, you want to be ready to R.A.C.E.: *Rested, Alert, Comfortable,* and *Energetic!*

Chapter 2 | **Writing About a Picture**

Thinking and Prewriting   5–7 minutes

Writing   18–20 minutes

Editing   5 minutes

This question asks you to write a story about a picture.

**30
Minutes**

OVERVIEW: HOW WILL IT LOOK?

The first task on Day 1 of the New Jersey HSPA in Language Arts Literacy is a 30-minute extended writing in response to a picture. The general directions for this task have been reprinted on page 6. Take a moment to become familiar with them.

Today you are going to take part of the High School Proficiency Assessment for Language Arts Literacy. The assessment contains different types of text and different activities. In the first part of the test, you will look at a picture and then complete a writing task. In this activity, you have an opportunity to demonstrate how well you can organize and express your ideas in written text. You have received a Writer's Checklist of important points to remember as you write. Educators who read your writing will consider these important points when they read and score your writing.

You will have 30 minutes to complete the writing task. Take a few minutes to think about the task and to plan what you want to say before you begin to write. You may use the prewriting/planning space to plan your text, but your prewriting will not be scored. **Only your writing in your answer folder will be scored.** Do your best to make your writing clear and well organized. Keep your purpose in mind as you write and use your checklist.

You must use a No. 2 pencil. You may either print or write your final copy. You may not use a dictionary or any other reference materials during the test. However, you may use the Writer's Checklist. If you finish before the time is called, review what you have written, using the Writer's Checklist to read critically and improve what you have written. Then close your test booklet and wait quietly until you receive further instructions.

Decision: Before you take the test, decide whether you are going to print or write in cursive. You may write in either to record your response. However, one of the criteria on the Writer's Checklist is to write neatly.

It is important that the graders be able to read what has been written, and graders are predisposed to favor responses that they do not have to struggle through because of the handwriting. So, **make a decision now**. Use whichever form of writing is the neatest and take all the practices using that form.

WHAT ARE YOU BEING ASKED TO DO?

The picture response gives 30 minutes to prewrite, write, and edit. It also gives room to be creative—but only to think creatively, not to write in any form you choose. The response needs to be structured and well written. You are given general instructions, the picture, the question, one blank page for prewriting, and two lined pages for your response. There is not a lot of time, so the approach and the response need to be focused.

The Picture and the Question

On the page after the general directions will be the picture and the question. The directions will <u>end</u> by asking that you

"Use your imagination and experience to speculate about what is happening. Then write your story."

The question will have a few introductory sentences, depending on the picture, so there may be variations in the first sentences. These sentences will usually give some additional information to use in your writing, but this information will be very general. As you will see in the writing section, the information may be useful in the introduction.

The directions for the writing task will be printed below the picture. A sample picture and the directions for the writing task are shown here. Take a moment to become familiar with them.

Sample Picture Prompt and Question

Credit: bigfoto.com

An ancient proverb says, "A picture is worth a thousand words." Regardless of the artist's original intent, what we see in the picture can be very different from what others see. What story does this picture tell you? Use your imagination and experience to speculate about what is happening. Then write your story.

Speculate means to draw conclusions based upon careful consideration of available facts or other information. When you speculate, you use your knowledge, experience, and good judgment to come to a conclusion. In addition, when writing about the picture prompt, the writer should use his or her imagination.

You are being asked to use the picture to create a story about what is going on, and then to convey these ideas to the reader in a structured, written answer. There are no right or wrong answers, but the picture must be used as the basis for the response.

Credit: bigfoto.com

Approaches

- You could write about a myriad of ideas for this picture.
- You could write about practicing to accomplish a goal, or the joy of a moment.
- You could write about one of the musicians or about anyone in the crowd watching this performance!
  - Do not write about penguins.
  - Do not write about the latest movie you saw. Neither of these ideas has anything to do with the picture.
  - Do not go off on a tangent.

If the graders get a response that seems to have nothing to do with the picture, they will mark it OT (off topic) and you will not get credit for your answer.

This is not the time to make large, logical leaps and expect the reader to follow.

Words to Know
Take a few minutes to become familiar with these words that will help you discuss the picture.

Background: The background of a picture contains the farthest elements one can see in the picture. It is equivalent to the setting in a story. When writing about the background, discuss the surrounding area, the environment, and things you notice in the distance or at the horizon. Be aware that activities can be taking place in the background.

Foreground: The foreground of a picture contains the closest elements in the picture. These may be objects or people and usually are involved in some type of activity. The foreground consists of things you might "meet" if you were to step into the picture.

Figures: The figures are the people or animals that are in the picture. They may be doing something or focusing on something else in the picture. They can be considered the "main characters" of the picture.

Action: The action refers to what is actually happening at the moment the photo was taken. It is your "anchor." You must speculate on the cause of this moment and its effect.

HOW YOU "READ" A PICTURE: BREAKING IT DOWN AND ASKING YOURSELF QUESTIONS

Most of us think we should be able to look at a picture and easily discuss it, and in many cases we can. Yet, using a picture as a basis for writing is different. The first task is to decide what information the picture gives you. Some pictures focus on the <u>foreground</u> of the picture to give information, as in the picture on this page. Some pictures, like the one in the first sample, use the <u>background</u> of the picture to help you understand what is going on. The first step in getting information is to break the picture down into its background and foreground. Can you identify the background and the foreground in the pictures below?

Background

_____

_____

_____

Foreground

_____

_____

_____

READING THE PICTURE

Look at the picture. Now cover the people with your hand or a piece of paper so that you are looking at just the background. Now answer these questions:

READING THE BACKGROUND

Place (where)

Where do I think this is?

_____

(A city, a farm, the desert, the mountains? Is this in another part of the world?)

Background Action (when)

What is happening? (Sometimes there is nothing except scenery, and sometimes there is something going on.)

_____

_____

READING THE FOREGROUND

Now take the paper or your hand away and look at the figures in the foreground of the picture.

Foreground Action

What is there?

_____

What is happening?

_____

_____

Is the foreground the same as the background or is it different?

_____

```
┌──────────────┐
│ What         │
│              │
│              │
└──────┬───────┘
       │
       ▼
┌──────────────┐      ┌──────────────┐      ┌──────────────┐
│ Where        │ ───▶ │ When         │ ───▶ │ Why          │
│              │      │              │      │              │
│              │      │              │      │              │
└──────────────┘      └──────────────┘      └──────────────┘
```

Figures

If there is a person in the picture, what is the person doing? (Or what are the people doing?)

_____

_____

If you can see the expression on the characters' faces, how would you characterize that expression? (shocked, happy, sad, worried, bored, etc.)

_____

_____

Now write two sentences about the background.

_____

_____

_____

_____

Write two sentences about the foreground.

_____

_____

_____

_____

How do the background and the foreground go together?

_____

_____

_____

_____

What do you think happened just before this picture was taken?

_____

_____

_____

_____

What do you think is going to happen next?

_____

_____

_____

_____

Once you have answered these questions, you have thought through the question and are ready to prewrite. On the actual test you will not write out the answers to these questions; you will be able to answer these in your mind. But to accomplish this, you need to practice. You may find that writing the answers on the prewriting/planning sheet will help you stay focused.

PRACTICE: READING THE PICTURE

Credit: bigfoto.com

Background

Place—Where do I think this is?

_____

_____

_____

_____

Backgrond Action—What is happening?

_____

_____

_____

_____

Foreground

What is there?

_____

_____

_____

_____

Is the foreground the same as the background or is it different?

_____

_____

_____

_____

FOREGROUND ACTION

What is the person (people) doing?

_____

_____

_____

_____

What is the expression on the character'(s) face(s)?

_____

_____

_____

_____

Write two sentences about the background.

_____

_____

_____

_____

Write two sentences about the foreground.

_____

_____

_____

_____

How do the background and foreground go together?

_____

_____

_____

_____

What do you think happened just before this picture was taken?

_____

_____

_____

_____

What do you think is going to happen next?

_____

_____

_____

_____

PREWRITING: FIVE MINUTES THAT CAN MAKE A DIFFERENCE!

Thinking about a picture and then taking a few minutes to prewrite is a way to help your essay organization. Here are a few prewriting strategies you can try. They will help you think about a picture so that you can create an organized story in answer to the writing task. Once you decide which one you prefer, use that method as you practice all of the picture prompts.

Method 1

Look carefully at the picture and pretend that you were there the moment it was taken. Now, use your imagination and decide which of the following roles you might play:

1. Are you the photographer?
2. Are you a person walking by watching the picture being taken?
3. Are you one of the characters in the picture?

After you determine the role you will play, quickly jot down some words that answer the following questions:

In my role as _____ what sounds do I hear?

_____

In my role as _____ what things do I smell?

_____

In my role as _____ what things do I feel?

_____

Now, jot down a few other details, and you are ready to start your story!

1. When do I think this takes place? (Past? Present? Future?)

   _____

2. Where do I think this takes place?

   _____

3. What are three important details from the picture that I will use in my story?

   a. _____

   b. _____

   c. _____

Method 2

Look carefully at the picture and at the character(s) in the photograph. Now, use your imagination as you think about the person or people in the picture:

1. What are his/her/their names?

   _____

2. Why are they in the picture?

   _____

3. What is happening?

   _____

4. Why is this happening?

   _____

5. What is going to happen next?

   _____

6. What three important details from the picture will you use to prove your prediction?

   a. _____

   b. _____

   c. _____

Now, begin your story using the answers to the above questions. Make sure to use the details you identified within the story.

Method 3

This is a graphic organizer; those of you who are more visual might find this an easier prewriting strategy.

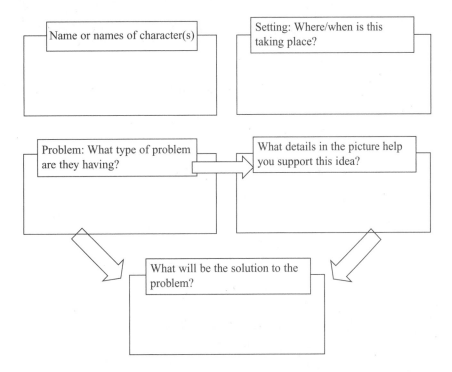

After filling in this organizer, you will be ready to begin your story!

The time spent prewriting will be extremely important. Once the basic ideas are structured, you can spend the rest of the time concentrating on the actual writing of the piece.

Before we move on to the final writing, try a few exercises with the first two steps: reading the picture and prewriting. You should time yourself. REMEMBER, you will have approximately 5–7 minutes on the actual test to get through this phase; if you take longer, you may not have time to edit.

Answer questions about picture.

Which one of these methods will you use to talk about this picture?

Method 1 (putting yourself into the photo)
• Who are you in the photo?
• What do you hear/smell/feel?
• Where/when is this taking place?
• What details will you use?

Method 2 (putting someone into the picture and building a story)
• Create a name for your character/characters
• Why are they there?
• What is happening?
• What is going to happen next?
• What details will you use?

Method 3 (graphic organizer)
• Character(s) names
• Setting
• Problem
• Details that support this idea
• Solution

Here are a few beginning sentences using each method. Compare these to your own effort.

Method 1 (putting yourself into the photo)

It was a cold, crisp, December day. I could smell fires burning in my neighbors' fireplaces as I walked into Woodmore Park. My hands were freezing and my eyes were watering with the cold. I wrapped my scarf more tightly around my neck and halfway around my face. My new skates hung over my shoulder and I could not wait to try them out on the frozen pond. It was then that I saw the sign!

Method 2 (putting someone into the photo and building a story)

Jack and John were "friendly" competitors. They competed for grades at school and they competed at sports. It was not a surprise to anyone that when both boys got new skates for Christmas they would want to race each other at the local pond.

The date and time of the big race had been set for weeks. The boys planned to meet at Woodmore Park and race across the pond to the other side. Both boys were excited. Saturday, January 18th would be an exciting day and would finally prove which one was the faster skater! As they drove into the park the tension was palpable. It was then that they saw the sign!

Method 3 (Graphic Organizer—character, setting, problem, . . .)

Jillian loved winter because she could spend hours on the frozen pond at Woodmore Park. "Today is perfect," thought Jillian as she tied on her skates. The sun was out, the air was crisp, and the park was quiet. It wasn't until she was midway across the ice that she saw the sign!

WRITING YOUR PAPER

This prompt is asking you to write a story based on the picture, using the information in the picture as a basis for the story. However, the story is graded using the New Jersey Registered Holistic Grading Rubric. The rubric is based upon structure, organization, mechanics, and usage. Once you have "read the picture" and done the prewriting, you are ready to write an interesting story. Editing is necessary when finished.

The story must have a distinct beginning, middle, and end. Because it is almost impossible to write a story without these three elements, you should find yourself automatically complying with these criteria. However, students who are accomplished creative writers should be aware that stream-of-conscious or poetic forms will not satisfy the criteria for this task. You have been asked to write a story, and this is the form that must be used.

- The story should use the information gathered from the picture to establish the "setting."
- The story should use the information gathered from the picture to establish the "characters." (Consider making yourself one of the characters to tie some of your experience into the story.)
- You do not have to establish a tremendous conflict; you do not have the writing time to follow a formal rising action, climax, and falling action development. Your story is more a "slice of life."

- The steps of the plot should be fairly simple. Do not attempt to weave an extremely complex tale; there is not time to develop it properly. Simply take the action or situation in the picture and develop what happened before the picture was taken, what is happening, or what will happen after the picture.

Writing the Beginning

It is helpful to begin with the setting—a basic description of what is going on in the picture. This allows you to set the tone of the piece and to start writing from "the known." Introduce characters in this section of the story.

Writing the Middle

The next section of the story should be from the prewriting "what is going to happen next." Use imagination to develop what you have established in the prewriting.

Writing the Ending

The end of the story should be clear. There should be some resolution to the conflict, or the story should give the reader room to speculate about what is going to happen next.

REVISING AND EDITING

Writer's Checklist

Before you begin the writing tasks you will be given a "Writer's Checklist." This is a summary of the writing elements at which the graders are looking. After you have finished writing your story, go back and read your paper checking off each item on the Writer's Checklist.

Example of elements on the HSPA Writer's Checklist:

Content/Organization

_____ Focus: the essay has one clear focus and does not contain irrelevant items.

_____ Development of central idea: the main idea is logically developed.

_____ Support of central idea: the main idea is supported by examples, details, and logical explanations.

_____ Order: the development of the central idea is in logical order.

Sentence Construction

_____ Sentence patterns are varied and fit the idea.

Usage

_____ Words are used correctly. (Do NOT use SAT vocabulary if you do not know how the word functions in a sentence.)

Mechanics

_____ Correct capitalization, spelling, and punctuation.

_____ Legible writing.

The additional elements on the Writer's Checklist are generally on the back of the sheet you are given. These include:

_____   A clear introduction and conclusion

_____   Transitions between paragraphs and ideas

_____   Varied sentence structure

_____   Correct subject/verb agreement

_____   Correct verb tenses

_____   Correct pronoun/pronoun antecedent agreement

How Are You Scored?

Here is a sample of the rubric for this writing task. Chapter 1 explains what a rubric is and how it will be used. Two readers will read your story that you have written about a picture and score your writing according to the New Jersey Holistic Scoring Rubric. Six points is the maximum score that any one reader can give your paper. The scores of the two readers will then be *averaged* and that number will be your score on this task.

There are four possible reasons that you would get a 0 (non-scorable response):

1. FR—fragment
    (You did not write enough for the graders to score the piece)
2. OT—off topic, off task
    (You did not respond to the question but wrote about something else. You wrote a short story, not a persuasive essay. You wrote a dialogue.)
3. NE—not English
    (You wrote the majority of the essay in a language other than English)
4. WF—wrong format
    You did not write a story for this task.

The graders are looking for the following:

1. There is a distinct opening and closing
    (Each should be a paragraph—that makes it easy to see that you do have an opening and closing.)
2. Each supporting paragraph is well-developed and is clearly linked to other paragraphs. All support your main idea.
3. Details are effective, vivid, explicit, and/or pertinent.
4. The ideas are not just thrown together but are logically placed to build your case.
5. You have effectively used an analogy, simile, metaphor or other rhetorical device, considered a "compositional risk." You have demonstrated that you can control language.
6. There are few errors in wording or sentence structure that "stop" the reader.
7. Sentence structure is varied enough that it is not boring and repetitive.
8. Spelling, capitalization, and punctuation are correct. (If you have spelled one word incorrectly it is not a problem. If you have spelled one word incorrectly and repeat that word 15 times in the essay, it is a problem.)

The actual New Jersey Holistic Scoring Rubric is available at the back of this book <u>or</u> online at the New Jersey Department of Education Web Site.

PUTTING IT ALL TOGETHER: SAMPLE PICTURE PROMPT WRITING TASKS

Directions for Practice 1–6: An ancient proverb says, "A picture is worth a thousand words." Regardless of the artist's original intent, what we see in pictures can be very different from what others see. What stories do these pictures tell you? Use your imagination and experience to speculate about what is happening. Then write your story.

Practice 1

Credit: bigfoto.com

_____

_____

_____

_____

_____

_____

_____

_____

_____

_____

_____

_____

_____

_____

_____

_____

_____

_____

_____

_____

_____

_____

_____

_____

_____

_____

_____

_____

_____

_____

_____

Credit: bigfoto.com

_____

_____

_____

_____

_____

_____

_____

_____

_____

_____

_____

_____

_____

_____

_____

_____

Chapter 3 | **Reading and Responding to a Narrative Passage**

OVERVIEW: WHAT IS A "NARRATIVE PASSAGE" AND HOW WILL IT LOOK?

For the HSPA, a *narrative passage* is defined as literature written to tell a story. The passages you will be asked to read are selected from previously published literature. They will be between 2,100 and 3,300 words in length with numbers in the margins to identify certain paragraphs. The selections can come from various sources and may be excerpts (parts) from a longer work, or they may be complete works. The selections have all been chosen because they have specific, common elements. The following is a list of the elements that may be found in the narrative selections chosen for this assessment:

- The selection will have a clearly established problem/conflict and a resolution to that problem.
- The selection will follow a traditional narrative structure with an organized plot and well-developed characters.
- The setting will be important to the plot and to the characters.
- The reading selection will use a range of literary devices such as imagery, foreshadowing, flashback, and figurative language.
- The selection will contain vocabulary for which adequate context clues are provided.
- The selection will allow readers to think about universal themes and diverse cultures and perspectives.

The remainder of this chapter discusses these key elements of narrative writing and presents an opportunity to practice important strategies so that you can become a careful, thoughtful reader.

Each narrative reading selection has a brief introduction in bold print before the title and author of the selection. This introduction can provide some very important information and should be read! It may tell what the selection is about, whether it is an excerpt or a complete work, and may even indicate the author's purpose for writing. It will "set the stage" if it is part of a larger work, and can often give ideas about the setting, time frame, or plot. These few sentences help you prepare for what you are about to read and can be very helpful in answering some of the multiple-choice questions afterward. If there is a title to the selection, take note of that before beginning to read.

Immediately following the narrative selection are ten multiple-choice questions and two open-ended questions. These are explained fully in the rest of this chapter. You will have a total of 50 minutes to complete the reading and answer the multiple-choice and open-ended questions. Answer the multiple-choice questions by filling in the correct circle on the answer sheet. The lined paper in the separate answer booklet is for answering the open-ended questions.

The directions for this part of the HSPA in Language Arts Literacy HSPA will look like this:

Directions:

In this part of the test, you will read a narrative passage and then respond to the multiple-choice and open-ended questions that follow it. You may look back at the passage and make notes in your test booklet if you like, but you must record your answers in your answer folder.

You will have 50 minutes for this part of the test. If you finish this part before the time is called, close your test booklet and wait quietly until you receive further instructions.

The page containing the narrative passage will have further directions telling you to read the passage and record answers to the multiple-choice questions in the answer folder. Next will follow the "introductory" sentences as described above. The reading selection will be organized in two columns and indicate to "go on to the next page" until the passage is finished.

GO ON ➡

WHAT ARE YOU BEING ASKED TO DO?

Reading is a complex process that asks you to use reading skills, prior knowledge, ability to analyze, and ability to understand, in order to connect with an author's ideas. On the "Reading and Responding to a Narrative Passage" section of the HSPA, you are asked to read a given selection and answer ten multiple-choice and two open-ended questions about the reading. The multiple-choice questions and the open-ended questions are designed to assess your ability to interpret, critique, and analyze the content and meaning of a given text. Some or all of the following specific skills will be assessed for each HSPA reading selection through the multiple-choice and open-ended questions:

1. Recognizing central ideas and/or themes
2. Recognizing supporting details
3. Extrapolation of information/following directions
4. Paraphrasing/retelling
5. Recognizing how a text is organized
6. Recognizing the author's intended purpose
7. Questioning
8. Making predictions of tentative meanings
9. Forming opinions
10. Drawing conclusions
11. Interpretation of textual conventions and literary elements

The reading strategies that follow discuss each of these skills in detail, and the sample reading passage at the end of this chapter indicates the specific skill or skills associated with each multiple-choice question. This will help identify specific strategies that may require further practice to succeed on the HSPA.

READING STRATEGIES FOR NARRATIVE PASSAGES

As discussed in the opening of this chapter, there are specific requirements for reading selections that will be chosen for the HSPA in Language Arts Literacy. These readings will have elements that are common to most narrative literature. As you read the selection on the HSPA, make certain to keep your pencil in your hand. Freely underline, highlight, or take note of words, phrases, or ideas that seem to be important to the selection. On this test you ARE allowed to write in the test booklet—just don't put stray marks on the answer booklet.

Let's take a moment to examine those elements that may be found in a given narrative selection:

1. The selection will have a clearly established problem/conflict and a resolution to that problem.

The problem or conflict presented in a reading selection is generally centered on either the plot or the characters, sometimes both. The problem/conflict is what makes characters act or react and usually what sets the plot in motion. Something exists or something happens that needs to be changed or reacted to, and this usually establishes the problem or conflict in a piece of literature.

The actions taken to solve that conflict or problem produce a resolution. Sometimes a specific choice made by a character can solve the conflict; at other times it is simply fate, or nature, or uncontrolled elements that bring about the solution.

Every selection read will have a different problem or conflict, and there are as many ways to resolve that problem as there are authors! Part of the fun of reading is trying to figure out how a given problem may be solved; sometimes you will not agree with the actions taken to solve it. As you actively engage in reading, you will often form your own opinions as to how a conflict might have been resolved. There may be the opportunity to discuss how YOU might have solved a given conflict when writing answers to the open-ended questions that appear after a reading selection.

2. The selection will follow a traditional narrative structure with a well-organized plot and well-developed characters.

A "traditional" narrative structure means that as you read a given selection, a "story" unfolds; you meet and learn about certain characters, their problems, their lives, and their motivations for certain actions. A narrative selection will probably require inference to understand some elements of the plot or characters. For example, if an author says that a particular character "avoided eye contact," ask yourself, based on what you have been told about that character, if he or she is shy, or embarrassed, or trying to hide something.

If an author presents well-developed characters, you might learn why they are motivated in a certain way, why they react as they do, or why they choose to act or react to a given element in the plot. You will be able to mentally "sketch" the character: how he or she might look, whether he or she is sad, happy, lonely, angry, or bored. Given certain traits of that character, you will sometimes be able to guess what he or she is going to do even before it occurs in the plot! Pay close attention to the author's descriptions—highlight or underline specific words or phrases that help you "see" the character or understand something special about the character.

A well-organized plot will move the reader from one action to another with a specific purpose. Generally the plot will build so that the "climax" or high point is a realization or action toward which everything has been moving. Once the climax is reached, there is a "resolution" (see #2 above) where elements of the plot or characters fall into place based on a particular action or reaction.

3. The setting will be important to the plot and characters.

Setting is the time and place in which the events of the story take place. The author of any narrative piece chooses his or her setting for a specific purpose. Often the introduction helps to identify the specific setting of a selection, so make certain to pay attention to the sentences above the title. Sometimes language helps identify a setting. For example, if a character is using words such as "thou" or "shall," you might guess that the setting is in the past. If the character or characters are using words from another language, you may be able to place the country in which the story takes place. Sometimes elements in a given setting are what causes the conflict or problem, or what helps resolve an issue.

4. The reading selection will use a range of literary devices such as imagery, foreshadowing, flashback, and figurative language.

See the glossary at the end of this chapter for a list of the most commonly used literary devices.

5. The selection will contain a range of vocabulary for which adequate context is provided.

If you can understand the meaning of a sentence, even if there are unfamiliar words, continue reading. You are reading for overall meaning. If the test asks about a specific word in the multiple-choice section, return to the passage and use the context clues to figure out the word's specific meaning.

Often on the HSPA reading selection, words will be marked with an asterisk(*) and defined at the bottom of the page. If you see an asterisk, be sure to read the associated note.

6. The selection will allow readers to think about universal themes and diverse cultures and perspectives.

A universal theme is an idea that is generally true for all people at all times. It is a point of human nature or human interaction that has been observed for centuries. Some examples of universal themes might be parents' desires to produce better lives for their children, the individual's desires for peace, tranquility, fame, or fortune, or the illusion that money and power produce happiness.

Because universal themes apply to all people at all times, the HSPA reading selection may provide an opportunity to read about people of different cultures, ethnicities, or religions. The selection may present perspectives that are different from those you have experienced.

MULTIPLE-CHOICE QUESTIONS: STRATEGIES FOR PICKING THE RIGHT ANSWER

The ten multiple-choice questions that follow each reading passage on the HSPA test a variety of reading and thinking skills. There are two basic types of multiple-choice questions on the test: one poses a question and asks you to select an answer, and the other begins a sentence and asks you to choose the correct completion to that sentence. No matter which type of question posed, you will be given a choice of four possible answers.

Question and Answer:

1 Which of the following is an example of a metaphor?
   A She sings like a bird.
   B He was short and wore glasses.
   C The fire danced in the darkness.
   D She was a butterfly as she moved among the crowd.

Sentence Completion:

2 Donald tells Jennings a striper is "not as good as a shark" because
   A he has plans to claim Jennings' fish as his own.
   B he wants Jennings to feel inferior to him.
   C he wants to encourage Jennings to fish again.
   D he enjoys making fun of Jennings.

How do you pick the correct answer? Naturally, there are no surefire guarantees, but a few helpful hints can guide you and at least help narrow the possible responses.

1. Make sure to read the question carefully! Understand what is being asked and take note of any key words or phrases.
   • A key word may be in *italics,* **bold**, or even <u>underlined</u>. Sometimes key words are in all capital letters.
   • Key words such as *most, best, most likely, might, although,* or *often* imply that more than one answer may fit, but try to look for the answer that most closely fits the category.
   • Key words can also help narrow down the answers. For example, questions that are phrased with specific key words will help limit your choices:

   The author's <u>main point</u> is . . .

   One example of <u>understatement</u> would be . . .

   The main <u>theme</u> . . .

   The narrator's <u>tone</u> is best described as . . .

   All of these key words can signal you as you search for an answer.

2. For multiple-choice selections that are question/answer types of items, read the question and try to answer it <u>before</u> you read through the answers. If a similar answer is there, it is most probably the correct response. Always read through the other answers to make certain the one you have chosen is the best response.

   For multiple-choice selections that are sentence-completion types of items, try to finish the sentence before you look at the answers. Next, read the complete sentence with each possible item before you make a final selection. Choose the one that best completes the sentence.

3. Remember to USE THE TEXT to help select your answers. Oftentimes, a question will refer to a specific line or paragraph in the reading selection. Turn back to that section to help answer the question. Remember, the HSPA is assessing whether you are a careful, thoughtful reader, so think about what you are reading, use context clues where needed, and be sure you understand the question before choosing an answer.

    For vocabulary questions, always go back and reread the sentence. Substitute the choices into the sentence to help determine which word works best in the sentence context.

4. Remember, you have a limited time to complete the reading selection, the multiple-choice questions, and the open-ended questions. Therefore, work at a focused and constant pace. If you get stuck on a question, don't spend too much time with it. Try to eliminate as many responses as possible, then make a choice from the remaining answers. **Answer each and every question on this test.**

    Every multiple-choice question is worth one point. You are not penalized for getting an answer wrong, so it pays to try to guess. If time is remaining at the end of the test, go back to a question and try to work it out.

    Earlier in this chapter, you were told that the multiple-choice and open-ended questions are meant to assess certain specific skills. Naturally, because skills in language arts overlap one another (reading, writing, speaking, thinking, etc.), questions are designed to show that you are an active and thoughtful reader and writer. The following section explains the skills that will be called upon for the HSPA and offer some strategies you might use to practice them.

Recognizing Central Ideas and/or Themes

The central idea or theme of a given selection is the main focus of a piece of writing. It is the main idea that the author wants the reader to understand. In a narrative piece of writing authors often use characters, plots, actions, and a wide variety of literary techniques to present their central ideas to the reader. Narrative literature often uses figurative language such as metaphors and similes, symbols, imagery, and a variety of motifs to highlight the central idea or theme. In narrative writings a reader must "read between the lines" and be able to use inferences to understand the main theme, as it is not usually presented in a direct way.

To help recognize the main theme or central idea of a narrative selection, you will need to think about what the author has said through the characters, plot, and literary techniques. Oftentimes, the lesson learned by a specific character or the way a plot is resolved can indicate the main theme of the writing. Sometimes the author uses a repeating symbol—a bird, for example, or a specific color, or unusual lighting—to reinforce a central theme.

Don't overlook the importance of the title, the introduction, or an author's footnotes. Sometimes they can help the reader understand and even identify the central idea of a selection.

As you read, underline words, phrases, or ideas that are intriguing, are repeated, or that strike you in some specific way. At the end of the selection you will often see that these lead you to understand the author's theme.

Recognizing Supporting Details

Words are organized into sentences and sentences are organized into paragraphs. Paragraphs are groups of sentences about a single topic. The main idea of each paragraph can be found in its topic sentence. (Sometimes that main idea is not stated, but implied.)

In addition to a topic sentence, paragraphs contain other sentences, which through facts, details, examples, and logic support that topic sentence. Just as sentences in paragraphs add details to that paragraph, whole paragraphs usually add supporting details to the main theme or central idea of the entire narrative.

Supporting details in narrative selections usually add to character, plot, or theme development. In persuasive writings, supporting details usually give examples, facts, statistics, and other information to support the main idea of the writing. Supporting details most often give the who, what, where, when, why, and how of a given selection. You may have to "search" for these in a narrative piece of literature; they are more obvious in a persuasive selection.

Extrapolation of Information/Following Directions

Extrapolation means being able to draw out certain information from a text. It shows that you can "read between the lines" and understand why certain things have been said. This skill, combined with "following directions," will often be assessed through the open-ended questions.

Paraphrasing/Retelling

A careful, focused reader should be able to paraphrase or say in his or her own words what has occurred in a given text. This skill asks that you understand something well enough to rephrase it on your own.

Sometimes, when a multiple-choice question seems overly difficult, it will help if you paraphrase the question. This will clarify what the question is asking.

Recognizing How a Text Is Organized

All texts have a beginning, a middle, and an end, although authors of narrative texts have more flexibility and can be creative in unusual ways. Nevertheless, think about the way an author organized his or her words—think about setting, type of narrator, perspective, audience, use of dialogue, and other narrative techniques used by writers. Sometimes an author uses the technique of flashback—and the narration goes back in time or returns to the present at the end of the story. An author writes and rewrites to find the exact word, the exact phrase, and the perfect description to include in his or her work. All of these choices add up to aid the writer in creating and organizing a piece of literature.

You may have to infer the reason for a particular organizational pattern. Organization of persuasive texts is discussed in Chapter 5 of this book.

Recognizing the Author's Intended Purpose

Every author has a reason for writing. That reason may be to inform, to entertain, to explain, to influence, to imagine, to describe, to propose, or to present an entirely new perspective on something. As an advanced and active reader, it is important to recognize an author's intended purpose. In narrative selections, think about all of the "pieces" (plot, theme, character) and try to understand how they relate to one another. Examine what the author is saying through the characters and actions, and figure out what the author is implying.

Questioning

As an active reader, you should have certain questions forming in your mind. Those questions—Who? What? Why? Where? When? How?—should help you interact with the text. Jot these and other questions in the margins. Questions lead you to think about a given selection and most often lead to new perspectives and still further questions.

Making Predictions of Tentative Meanings

All of you have read materials in which you did not recognize or understand every single word or phrase. Nevertheless, you were able to understand what the selection was about. That is because we can often determine meanings by *context*—that is, the words or phrases surrounding the part we don't know. Certain clues help us figure out these new or strange meanings. Sometimes, we are helped by the ideas that surround the word, sometimes by a part of the word (prefix, suffix, or root), and sometimes by the part of speech the word must be (usually we know if something is a verb or a noun by context). At other times, we use our ability to infer to guess the probable meaning. The HSPA multiple-choice questions will often require you to guess at the meaning of a word. Certain strategies might be used to help accomplish this task:

- Although you might not know the specific word, go back to the text and observe the context in which it is used. Authors often elaborate on an idea by explaining it or by giving further details about it. These can help you understand the meaning of a word.
- Sometimes an author further defines a word by using words you do know. Read the sentence in which the unknown word appears, but also read several sentences before and after it. These will help give you context clues.
- Oftentimes, the examples provided after the unknown word or phrase can trigger your understanding.
- An antonym (opposite word) or synonym (similar word) in a nearby sentence can also help you identify your unknown word.
- Finally, remember to try to identify what part of speech the word may be. This can help if you have to guess at a multiple-choice answer. Try putting a noun in its place; if it "works," the mystery word is probably a noun (or a verb, adjective, adverb, etc.).

Forming Opinions

When you read, you naturally form opinions: about characters, about motivations, about ethical questions, about specific actions, or resolutions. An active reader should be able to form opinions based on a given reading. However, opinions should be based on information; when the HSPA assesses the ability to "form opinions," it means that the reader can read, react to the reading, and make an informed judgment supported by textual information. Make certain to refer to the text and use supporting evidence when you state your opinions.

Drawing Conclusions

A careful reader is also able to draw conclusions from a reading selection. In a narrative work it is often a conclusion based on the ability to infer. When you draw conclusions, use textual information to support your position. When asked to draw a conclusion, there will often not be "one" correct response; the response need only be based on the information and materials found in the reading selection. You will often be asked to draw conclusions as part of the open-ended writing tasks. As you read a selection and attempt to draw a conclusion or make inferences about the meaning, it is important to examine the work to determine how all of the information, supporting details, events, and characters connect to one another logically. A conclusion will be based on the sum of all of the elements working together in the story.

Interpretation of Textual Conventions and Literary Elements

Textual conventions and literary elements are not limited to fictional writing; writers often combine techniques to suit their intended purpose. Nonfiction pieces often have numerous literary elements and figurative language, and fictional pieces borrow textual conventions from nonfiction all the time. The HSPA will ask questions to assess understanding of elements of fiction and nonfiction. These include elements of structure, imagery, figurative language, use of dialogue, techniques such as flashback, identification of mood, tone, setting, irony, and symbolism, to name but a few. You should maintain a list, with definitions, to become familiar with the meanings of these literary terms as you continue reading. A partial list with definitions is included at the end of this chapter.

OPEN-ENDED QUESTIONS: STRATEGIES FOR ANSWERING THESE QUESTIONS

Each open-ended question on the HSPA consists of a statement followed by two related questions. Each question is preceded by a bullet and is related to the other question in a variety of ways. Sometimes the first question requires you to formulate an opinion and the second question asks that you apply that opinion to a specific example. Sometimes the second question simply asks that you elaborate on the first response. Often, you are asked something specific about the text in the first question and then asked to make an inference in the second question. After each open-ended question you will be reminded to "use information from the text to support your response."

Open-ended questions are meant to be harder than the multiple-choice questions. There is no one right answer to these questions, but the grader wants to see a thoughtful and careful reader who is able to connect with the reading selection. How can you show this?

First, read the question carefully and understand exactly what is being asked of you. If the question asks you to choose *two* characters, make certain two are chosen. If the question asks you to identify *problems* of one of the characters, make certain to discuss more than one problem. As in the multiple-choice questions, open-ended questions will have words that help the reader key into exactly what is being asked. Pay particular attention to the wording of the question! Words such as *explain, identify, predict, analyze, state,* or *justify* are asking you to do something specific in your writing. Sometimes, words such as *how* (how does a character . . . how would an individual . . . how can . . .) should trigger an opinion or an inference.

Next, try to connect with the text by writing an insightful response to the question. Show that you understood the main point of the selection.

Most important, remember to use specific details and ideas from the selection to support your response.

How Long Should It Be?

Remember that your score does not reflect the length of the written response. You may write your answer in one or more paragraphs; decide how much to write and how to organize it based on your individual response. Some students write one paragraph, whereas others write several paragraphs for the same question. Most responses need to be at least four or five sentences to answer the question. More important than the length is whether you have answered all of the components to each question and whether you have shown understanding of both the task and the reading selection. One or two paragraphs may be enough for a particular question, but you may have to write more for another open-ended question.

HOW WILL YOU BE SCORED? SAMPLE RUBRIC FOR THE OPEN-ENDED WRITING TASK

The scoring rubric for the open-ended questions is based on a 4-point scale. That means that you can earn from 0 to 4 on these questions. There will be a total of four open-ended questions on the Language Arts HSPA: two after the narrative reading passage and multiple-choice questions, and two after the persuasive reading passage and multiple-choice questions. This means that for ALL the open-ended questions you could earn a possible total of 16 points.

Two readers will read each answer and the score will be an average of the points they award the response. A 0-point response means that the paper is off topic (the question has not been answered). A 4-point response means that you have understood the task, that you have completed all portions of the open-ended question (the bulleted items), and that you have given a thoughtful answer that connects with and uses the text. The rubric itself will look something like this:

Points	Criteria
4	The writer has understood the task, completed all bulleted requirements, and written a thoughtful, complete answer that is supported by the text material and may even extend the ideas in the text (goes beyond #3).
3	The writer has understood the task, completed all bulleted requirements, and written a response using ideas/information from the text for support.
2	The writer may have completed all of the bulleted requirements but shows only a partial understanding of the task and uses the text minimally so that his/her ideas are not supported very well.
1	The writer does not seem to understand the task, does not complete all of the bulleted requirements, and uses little if any of the text.
0	This response is off topic (has not attempted to answer the question).

Based upon this scoring rubric, it is important to answer each and every portion of the open-ended response and to use the text for support. Notice that this is the only way to receive a high score on the open-ended questions. You will be graded only on the criteria that is in the rubric: that means that spelling, mechanics, organization, and good opening and closing sentences are not as important as the criteria listed above. Realize that a strong opening, good supporting details, organization, and well-constructed sentences will make the response more readable and give the grader a favorable impression.

GLOSSARY OF LITERARY TERMS AND LITERARY DEVICES

Alliteration	The repetition of an initial consonant. "Then the _d_emon fell, that _d_welt in _d_arkness." (*Beowulf*)
Allusion	A reference to a commonly known event or piece of literature. He was, by all accounts, a combination of Robin Hood and Santa Claus; someone obviously too good to be real. (The use of both Santa Claus and Robin Hood tell the reader about the characteristics of the person because the stories are familiar.) Sandra Cisneros's essay "Straw into Gold" refers to the story "Rumpelstiltskin"; the title is an allusion.
Antagonist	The character or characters who are "against" the main character. (This is the "bad guy" in a story. The bad guy can be male or female.) The Klingons were the antagonists in the original *Star Trek* series.
Climax	The turning point of the action of the plot; the point in a story at which the reader has the greatest emotional response.
Conflict	Two opposing forces or ideas. The conflict usually is the basis for much of the action in the plot. There are basic conflicts (man versus man, man versus nature, man versus himself) and then there are conflicts that are specific to that particular story (Gary versus the teacher, Gary versus the bear, Gary trying to decide whether to go to school or to cut school).
Connotation	The way a word is used in everyday life; the associations that have been added to a word. Although the denotation of *net* is "anything that traps or ensnares," there are times when "*the Net*" is understood to mean the Internet. The connotation of the word in our society is different than its dictionary definition, and the meaning of the word depends upon the context of its use.
Denotation	The dictionary definition of a word or action. In the *net* example, the denotation of *net* is "anything that traps or ensnares." To remember the difference between connotation and denotation remember that denotation and dictionary both start with "d."
Dialogue	Conversation among characters, signified by quotation marks.
Flashback	The technique of presenting scenes or incidents that occurred before the opening scene of a work. *Their Eyes Were Watching God* starts at the end of the story and then "flashes back" to years before. *Ethan Frome* begins years after the accident and then "flashes back" to the time before the accident.
Foreshadowing	Giving clues to the reader about what is going to happen. In *The Scarlet Letter*, Dimmesdale's first speech gives the reader clues that he is more than just Hester's minister. In *Beowulf* the reader is told that good will triumph, which foreshadows Beowulf's victory over Grendel.
Hyperbole	Exaggeration for a specific effect. The exclamation "It must be a thousand degrees out" is an example of hyperbole. No one believes that it is actually 1,000 degrees outside, but the exaggeration makes the point that it is very hot.

Irony	Irony occurs when the result is the opposite or contrary to what the reader (or character) expects (the difference between reality and appearance).
	There are many different types of irony. The most commonly used types in testing are verbal irony, situational irony, and irony of fate.
	Verbal irony is a figure of speech in which what is said contrasts with the meaning. Teenagers who say "You're kidding" are using a form of verbal irony; they do not mean that you are playing a joke on them or telling them something that is not true, although that is what the words say. They mean something along the lines of "Yes, I know, and it's really ridiculous."
	Situational irony involves the plot and/or characters. It is when an event or action occurs that is the opposite of what the reader has been led to expect.
	Irony of fate is when the "gods" manipulate human beings for amusement. In *Romeo and Juliet* the message does not get to Romeo; this is irony of fate.
Metaphor	A comparison between two unlike things that does not use the words *like* or *as*.
	"Fame is a bee"—Emily Dickinson
	"All the world's a stage"—Shakespeare
Mood	The emotional attitude or feeling in any part of a given work. A mood can be sad, happy, nostalgic, etc.
Narrator	A character or entity who speaks directly to the reader or who tells the story.
Omniscient	This means all knowing and is usually used to define point of view. An omniscient narrator knows what the characters are thinking, feeling, or doing.
Oxymoron	Bringing together two contradictory terms, such as *jumbo shrimp*.
Paradox	Seemingly contradictory or absurd statements existing at the same time.
	"I am not solitary while I read and write, though nobody is with me."—Emerson
Personification	Giving human qualities to nonhumans.
	Example: The rose blushed.
Plot	The sequence of events in a story; what happens in a story.
Point of view	The perspective from which a story is told.
Protagonist	The main character of a story.
	Frodo is the protagonist in *The Lord of the Rings* trilogy.
	Harry Potter is the protagonist in the *Chamber of Secrets*.
Resolution	How things work out in a story.
Satire	Making fun of something or someone with sarcasm or humor.
	Jonathan Swift's work *Gulliver's Travels* is a satire.
	The Adventures of Huckleberry Finn satirizes many aspects of the society.
	Most of *Saturday Night Live* is a satire.

Setting	The time and place of a story.
	Star Trek takes place in outer space, sometime in the future.
Simile	A comparison of two, unlike things using *like* or *as*.
	Example: "Wagons moving across like centipedes."—Steinbeck
Suspense	Created by having clues yet not knowing how things will turn out.
	The Sherlock Holmes stories are filled with suspense. So are the stories by Edgar Allan Poe.
Symbol	Something that stands for something else or suggests an idea.
	Example: A rose could be a symbol for love or beauty.
Theme	The central idea of a story; the main point the author wants to convey to the reader.
Tone	The emotional attitude or feeling of the entire work.
Understatement	Something that is represented as less than it is.
	Example: She was thrown off balance when she was hit by the truck.

PUTTING IT ALL TOGETHER: SAMPLE NARRATIVE PASSAGE WITH MULTIPLE-CHOICE AND OPEN-ENDED QUESTIONS

The selection that follows gives you a chance to practice taking the portion of the HSPA that contains the narrative reading passage.

Allow yourself 50 minutes to read the selection and answer the multiple-choice and open-ended questions that follow.

Use the strategies learned in this chapter as you read the selection. Check your answers using the answer key at the end of this chapter. Take note of the skills that seem to be your weakest and review that section.

Reading: Narrative Text

Jennings Michael Burch has written an autobiographical account of his childhood placement in a series of orphanages and foster homes when his mother was too sick to care for him. Although young Jennings was the frequent target of verbal as well as physical abuse, he also discovered moments of joy, of love, of great strength, and of personal triumph. The excerpt that follows describes a lesson the eleven-year-old Jennings learns when Donald, the son in one of the foster families where Jennings is placed, has halfheartedly agreed to take Jennings fishing with him early in the morning.

They Cage the Animals at Night
By Jennings Michael Burch

1   "Hey! Get up if you're coming with me," Donald yelled.
2   I pulled my head from under the pillow.
3   "I'll be in the kitchen," he said. "Hurry up."
4   I staggered to my feet in a daze. I was still asleep. I had a battle with my left eye. It
5   kept closing on me. I needed some water to help me win. I flipped on the light of the
6   little bathroom.
7   "Egad!" It nearly blinded me.
8   I found the water and woke myself up.
9   "If this is what it's like to go fishin' . . . why does anyone go?" I mumbled.

10   I finished up in the bathroom and got dressed. I met Donald in the kitchen.

11   "If you want anything, get it," he snarled. "But hurry up!"

12   "No, I'm all right."

13   He picked up an old dented pail with one hand, and the fishing poles with the other.
14 He pushed open the pantry door with his foot.

15   "Let's go," he said as the door slammed behind him.

16   I glanced up at the kitchen clock before I slipped out the door. It read ten after four.
17 Wow! I thought. I was never up at this hour before. I was starting to get really excited about
18 my first time fishing.

19   "Are you sure the fish will be awake by now?" I asked.

20   "Fish don't sleep, stupid!"

21   "Never?"

22   "Never. They take naps once in a while, but they never sleep."

23   "Gee, I didn't know that. I wonder how they can stay awake so long?"

24   "Did you ever try to sleep underwater?" he asked.

25   We reached a rise in the road. The rest of the way was downhill. There at the bottom,
26 breaking the darkness of night, were dozens of tiny lights shimmering off the water. To my
27 left I saw a long string of green lights that seemed to stretch for miles.

28   "What's that?" I asked.

29   "What?"

30   "All those green lights."

31   "That's the Whitestone Bridge."

32   "Oh, wow. I never saw a bridge."

33   "You never saw a bridge? Where you been?"

34   "I don't know. I just wasn't anywhere around a bridge. That's all."

35   When we got to the bottom of the hill, I could see a long wooden pier jutting straight
36 out into the water. Our feet made a clomping sound against the old thick boards of the pier.
37 We reached the end and Donald set the pail down.

38   "This is it," he said.

39   "It's beautiful," I said.

40   "What?"

41   He looked out at what I was looking at and shrugged his shoulders. I stared out at the
42 shimmering lights against the water and the wide open space that lay in front of me. It is
43 beautiful, I thought.

44   Donald handed me a pole. "I'm not going to bother teaching you how to cast," he said.
45 "Just drop the line straight down."

46   He helped me unreel my line. I was fishing for the first time. I was very excited.

47   "I hope I catch something," I said.

48   "Well, don't expect much the first time," he said.

49   He filled the old pail by lowering it down to the water with a rope.

50   "What's the water for?" I asked.

51   "That's to put the fish in. Just in case we catch any. This way they stay fresh."

52   I stood by the wooden rail with one foot on top of the other and waited. Donald did the
53 same. As the morning sun began to rise, I could see more and more things. I saw a long
54 row of boats, all tied together.

55   "Look at all those boats," I said.

56   "Shhhh," Donald said with his fingers to his lips. "That's the marina," he whispered.

57   "Oh. That's where your father keeps his boat," I also whispered.

58   "That's right," he again whispered.

59   "Why are we whispering?" I asked.

60   "We'll scare the fish away if we don't," he said.

61   "Oh."

62   Donald's reel began to spin with a whine. "I got one!" he shouted.

63   I was so excited. His pole bent as the fish took his line. My eyes were wide open. He
64   reeled in the line and bent the pole. He did it again and again until he pulled up the fish
65   and swung it over to the pail.

66   "It's a shark!" I shrieked. "You caught a shark!"

67   I had seen sharks in the movies, so I knew what they looked like. But I always thought
68   they were bigger. This one was about ten inches long.

69   "It's a sand shark," he said. "I'll throw him back."

70   "No, don't do that!" I said. "I want him."

71   "But it's only a sand shark. I catch them all the time."

72   "Oh, but I want him. Can I have him?"

73   Donald chuckled slightly but didn't say anything. He unhooked the sand shark and
74   slipped him into the pail. I sat back on my heels and watched the fish swim around in the
75   pail.

76   "You better watch your line," he said.

77   "Oh, yeah." I jumped back to the rail. I was more determined now than ever. I wanted
78   to catch something, too.

79   Suddenly there was a tug at my line. "I got something!" I shouted.

80   "Hook him!" he ordered. "Pull up and hook him!"

81   I did. I pulled up hard and he was hooked. The reel spun in my hand. Donald shouted
82   orders to me and I followed. I dipped the pole down and reeled as I pulled it up. I did it
83   again and again. I'm sure I got his orders all backwards, but I got the fish. As I started to
84   pull him up, Donald grabbed hold of the line and helped. He pulled the line hand over hand
85   and landed the fish on the pier. It was really big. Much too big to fit in the pail.

86   "It's a striper," he said.

87   "A striper? Is that a good one?" I asked.

88   "Yeah, well, it's okay. It's not as good as a shark, but it's only your first time."

89   "Maybe next time I'll get a shark," I said.

90   "Yeah, maybe," Donald said as he started taking apart the fishing poles.

91   "Are we leaving?" I asked.

92   "Sure. We gotta go to school."

93   "Oh, yeah! I forgot. I sure wish we had more time," I said. "Maybe I could catch a
94   shark now."

95   "I got an idea," he said. "How much money do you have?"

96   "Money?" I patted my pockets. "I don't got no money."

97   "Oh, well." He went into deep thought.

98   "Well, what?" I asked. "What?"

99   He sighed a great sigh. "Since you're poor," he said, "I'll let you have the shark for
100   nothing."

101   "Really!" I said. "Oh, wow! Thank you." I looked into the pail at my shark.

102   "It's too bad you don't have anything to give me," he said. "You know . . . sort of like
103   a trade."

104   "Well . . ." I thought for a moment. "How about my striper? You can have my striper. I
105   know it's not as good as a shark, but . . ."

106   "Okay. Let's trade fish," he said. "You say you caught the shark and I'll say I caught
107   the striper."

108   "Is that all right to do?"

109   "Sure. It's done all the time. We went fishing together, didn't we?"

110   "Yeah."

111   "Well, then . . . I'll just tell everyone you caught the better fish. That's all."

112   Donald slung the striper over his shoulder and then lifted the poles.

113   "Come on," he said, "grab the pail."

114   I took up the pail with both hands and followed him off the pier. As I walked, I watched
115   my shark swimming around. I couldn't wait to show Martha, and tell some of the kids in
116   my class. We walked back up the hill toward the house. The pail kept getting heavier and
117   heavier.

118   "Hey, wait for me!" I called out.

119   He had gotten so far ahead of me, I thought I might not find the house if I lost him. I
120   nearly caught up to him, when he started walking again.

121   "Hey, wait for me."

122   "The house is right there," he said as he pointed up the road.

123   It was. I struggled with the pail, setting it down every so often. By the time I had got-
124   ten to the pantry door, Donald was long gone. I brought the pail and my shark into the
125   kitchen.

126   "Whatcha got there?" Martha asked as she peered into the pail.

127   "A shark! We caught a shark!"

128   "A shark! What you want with a shark? Ya can't eat 'em."

129   "Eat him! I don't want to eat him. I want to keep him.

130   You know, for a pet."

131   "A pet!" she chuckled. "Now I thinks I heard everything. A shark for a pet. Well, set
132   him down in the pantry and gets yourself ready for school. Donald is gonna show where
133   to get the bus."

134   I put the pail and my shark in the pantry and started down the hall for the bedroom. I
135   heard Martha laughing.

136   "Land sakes! What'll he think of next?"

137   Donald showed me where to catch my bus.

138   I climbed aboard and showed the driver my school pass. . . .

139   I got off the bus and walked up the hill to school. I went into the yard. The school yard
140   was filled with kids from all the different grades. Each grade had an area where they lined
141   up when the bell rang. I went to the area of my class. I sat at the base of the tall black fence
142   that boarded the yard and I watched the kids play. They were playing tag. Eddie Keegan
143   was playing with them.

144   Eddie was the boy who sat next to me in class. He was really the only one in school I
145   ever talked to outside of Sister Gerard. I borrowed paper from him sometimes, or asked
146   him the answer to a question I didn't know. He would always lend me the paper or answer
147   the question, but he never talked more than that. I guess he never really wanted to be
148   friends with me.

149   "Hey, Eddie!" I called as he ran past me.

150   He stopped and backed up to me. He kept his eye on the kid who was "It"—he didn't
151   want to get tagged. "Yeah?" he said.

152   "I went fishing this morning."

153   "Fishing! This morning?"

154   "Yep."

155   "Where?"

156   "In the water. Near the Whitestone Bridge," I said proudly.

157   He sort of looked at me funny. Like he didn't believe me.

158   "I did," I said. "I really did."

159   "Oh, yeah. What did you catch?"

160   "A shark!" I said. I knew he'd be impressed by that.

161   "A *shark!*"

162   "Uh-huh." I smiled.

163   "Hey, everybody!" he shouted to the others. "Listen to this. Burch caught a shark!"

164   The kids stopped playing tag and gathered around me.

165   "Burch went fishing this morning and caught a shark," Eddie told them.

166   I stood there proud and smiling, but not for long.

167   They started to laugh at me. None of them believed me.

168   "I did," I insisted. "I have him in a pail."

169   "A pail!" one of them laughed. "You put a shark in a pail?"

170   I was embarrassed. They laughed and laughed. They began to make fish faces at me
171   and call me a liar. I left the yard and went into school. I knew Sister Gerard was in the
172   classroom, so I stayed in the hallway just outside the door. I didn't want her to see me
173   crying.

174   *(Later that evening, Jennings returns to his foster home. Mr. Frazier, the father, talks*
175   *to Jennings at the dining room table):*

176   "I saw the shark on the porch, Jennings," Mr. Frazier said.

177   I beamed with excitement. I was sure Mr. Frazier would be proud of me.

178   "After dinner, I'll take you down to the bay and we'll throw him back."

179   I was shocked. My face showed it.

180   "We can't keep a shark in the house. He won't live."

181   "I tried to tell him he couldn't keep it," Donald added. "But what can you do? He's just
182   a dumb kid."

183   "Now, be nice," Mrs. Frazier said.

184   "A shark needs salt water, Jennings. He won't last in that pail."

185   "But—"

186   "Donald will take you fishing again, and he'll teach you how to catch a real fish. Like
187   the one he caught."

188   I glared at Donald. He put his face into his soup bowl. He made some slurping sounds.

189   "Better fish?" I said.

190   "Yes," Mr. Frazier said. "He'll teach you how to catch a better fish."

191   "We can go tomorrow," Donald said.

192   "No thanks."

193   "Don't you like fishing?" Mrs. Frazier asked.

194   "Yes, ma'am. But what good is going if you can't tell nobody you went?"

The above excerpt has been reprinted from *They Cage the Animals at Night* with the permission of the author, Jennings Michael Burch.

Reading: *Items for* They Cage the Animals at Night

MULTIPLE-CHOICE QUESTIONS

1 In line 4, Jennings says that he "had a battle with my left eye." In this context he means
   A he forgot to wear his glasses.
   B he is so tired he can hardly see.
   C he hit himself in the eye while sleeping.
   D his right eye is his better eye.

2 Donald may feel more worldly than Jennings, but the reader knows this is not so when
  A Donald identifies the Whitestone Bridge.
  B Donald does not teach Jennings how to cast the fishing line.
  C Donald tells Jennings that fish don't sleep but may take naps once in a while.
  D Donald whispers so he will not scare the fish.

3 Donald tells Jennings a striper is "not as good as a shark" because
  A he has plans to claim Jennings's fish as his own.
  B he wants Jennings to feel inferior to him.
  C he wants to encourage Jennings to fish again.
  D he enjoys making fun of Jennings.

4 Which of the following BEST supports the image of Jennings as lonely?
  A "Eddie was the boy who sat next to me in class." (line 144)
  B "I sat at the base of the tall black fence that boarded the yard and I watched the kids play." (lines 141–142)
  C "Hey everybody! . . . Burch caught a shark!" (line 163)
  D "I was embarrassed." (line 170)

5 At the end of the story, Jennings says he does not want to go fishing again because
  A he doesn't like to get out of bed so early.
  B he is not allowed to keep the shark as a pet.
  C he is afraid that the incident may be repeated.
  D he knows that no one will believe him if he catches a real fish.

6 Which line tells the reader when Jennings knows that Donald has taken advantage of him?
  A "I was shocked." (line 179)
  B "He's just a dumb kid." (lines 181–182)
  C "He'll teach you how to catch a better fish." (line 190)
  D "I beamed with excitement." (line 177)

7 Which of the following is *not* evidence that Mr. and Mrs. Frazier believe Donald's story about the fish?
  A Mrs. Frazier replies that "Donald will take you fishing again, and he'll teach you how to catch a real fish." (line 186)
  B Mr. Frazier tells Jennings, "After dinner, I'll take you down to the bay and we'll throw him back." (line 178)
  C When Donald says Jennings is a "dumb kid," Mrs. Frazier tells him to "be nice." (line 183)
  D Donald makes slurping sounds as he eats his soup.

8 Which of the following is an example of personification?
  A "Fish don't sleep, stupid!" (line 20)
  B "He pushed open the pantry door with his foot." (line 14)
  C "There at the bottom, breaking the darkness of night, were dozens of tiny lights shimmering off the water." (lines 25–26)
  D "As the morning sun began to rise, I could see more and more things." (line 53)

9 Jennings agrees to tell everyone he caught the shark because of all of the following except
  A Donald assures him that the shark is superior to the striper.
  B Donald tells him "it's done all the time."
  C he has seen sharks only in the movies and is excited to think he has caught one.
  D he knows the kids at school won't believe him unless they see the fish in the pail.

10 At the end of the story, Donald "put his face into his soup bowl" because
  A he loves Martha's soup and wants to eat every last drop.
  B he realizes that Jennings has figured out his trick.
  C he is embarrassed because his mother has yelled at him.
  D he doesn't want to have to take Jennings fishing again.

Directions for questions 11 and 12:	Write your response in the space provided in the answer folder. DO NOT WRITE ANY RESPONSES IN THE TEST BOOKLET.

11 New experiences, whether good or bad, can significantly affect our lives.
  • Identify an important lesson Jennings learns from his fishing expedition.
  • Describe one possible change in Jennings' personality as a result of this experience.

Use information from the story to support your response.

Write your response to this open-ended question on the lined pages that follow.

_____

_____

_____

_____

_____

_____

_____

_____

_____

_____

_____

_____

12 Jennings Michael Burch, the author of this piece, has often said that one act of kindness or one act of friendship would have made all the difference in the world to him as a young child.
  • Identify two instances in this story where things might have been different had someone "reached out in friendship" to young Jennings.
  • Explain how you might use the ideas in this story to teach students about tolerance or kindness.

Use information from the story to support your response.

Write your response to this open-ended question on the lined pages that follow.

_____

_____

_____

_____

_____

_____

_____

_____

_____

_____

_____

_____

_____

_____

_____

_____

_____

_____

_____

_____

Answer Key and Skills Analysis for They Cage the Animals at Night

1.	**B**	Skill #8	Making predictions of tentative meanings
2.	**C**	Skill #3	Extrapolation of information
3.	**A**	Skill #4	Paraphrasing/retelling
4.	**B**	Skill #1	Recognizing central ideas and/or themes
5.	**D**	Skill #6	Recognizing the author's intended purpose
6.	**C**	Skill #2	Recognizing supporting details
7.	**D**	Skill #10	Drawing conclusions
8.	**A**	Skill #11	Interpretation of textual conventions and literary elements
9.	**D**	Skill #3	Extrapolation of information
10.	**B**	Skill #10	Drawing conclusions

OPEN-ENDED RESPONSE COMMENTS

11.   Skill #1   3, 10

A response to this open-ended question should answer <u>both</u> bulleted questions. The first part should identify a lesson Jennings learns from this experience; one such lesson might be about trust or friendship. Another lesson might relate to his feelings when he is taunted by his classmates. Make certain to use examples from the text to prove your point.

The second part of this response would be to describe a change in his personality as a result of this experience. Perhaps you might see Jennings as becoming less trusting. You might also write about his relationship with Donald from this point forward. A third possibility might be to discuss his relationship with his classmates. Again, make certain to use examples from the text to support your response.

12.   Skill #3   6, 9, 10

A response to this open-ended question should answer <u>both</u> bulleted questions. First, you should identify <u>two</u> specific places in the story where a "friendship" might have occurred. This might relate to something with Donald treating Jennings as a friend or younger brother rather than as an inferior being. Perhaps you might discuss someone at school (perhaps Eddie) who might have stood up for Jennings rather than tease him. You might even have written about Martha or the Fraziers questioning Donald more closely and believing in Jennings.

When you answer the next part of this question, you should make it personal. Discuss how you might reach out to someone in your school, someone who is not usually befriended by other students. Perhaps you could write about beginning a "bully" awareness group, or just about standing up for someone being teased by others. Make sure to use the text as a basis for the writing.

Chapter 4 | **The Persuasive Writing Task**

OVERVIEW: HOW WILL IT LOOK?

This writing task is the longest piece of writing on the HSPA. There will be one hour to prewrite, write, and edit the essay. Because most high school classes last less than an hour, you have had practice completing this task in the allotted time.

> There is a separate Persuasive Writing Task Folder
> that is used for this writing activity.

The first page of the task gives general directions and will look something like this:

Directions:

In this part of the test you will complete a writing task that gives you an opportunity to demonstrate how well you can organize and express your ideas in written text. You have been provided with a Writer's Checklist that lists important points to remember while you write; the graders will consider these points as they read and score your writing.

You will have 60 minutes to complete this task. Take the first few minutes to think and plan what you want to write about. You may use the Prewriting/Planning space in your test booklet, but nothing that you write in this space will be scored. Keep both your audience and the purpose you are writing in mind. Try to keep your writing clear and well organized.

You must use a No. 2 pencil to write. You may either write or print your final copy. You may not use any reference materials other than the Writer's Checklist during the test. When you are finished writing, read over your work. Revise and edit to improve what you have written.

The Writer's Checklist may be in the test booklet or it may be separate and handed out with the Persuasive Writing Task Folder. If it is separate, be certain that you have received one. This checklist generally contains the following:

Content/Organization

    ✔ 1. Your focus should be on the purpose of your writing and the audience for whom you are writing.

    ✔ 2. You should support your point of view with specific details and evidence.

    ✔ 3. The order and structure of your ideas will help communicate your view.

Sentence Construction

    ✔ 1. Use varied sentence structure.
    ✔ 2. Check that you do not have sentence fragments.
    ✔ 3. Check that you do not have run-on sentences.

Usage

    ✔ 1. Choose your words carefully so that you convey the meaning clearly.
    ✔ 2. Check that words have been used in the correct context.

Mechanics

    ✔ 1. Capitalize, spell, and punctuate correctly.

Write Neatly!

This checklist is helpful as a revision guide. But remember, the graders cannot grade a piece they cannot read!

After reading the first page of general directions and looking at the Writer's Checklist, you will find specific directions for the writing task.

Write the essay in the Persuasive Writing Task Folder provided. The answer folder will provide four lined pages for this task. You will also have blank pages to use for prewriting/planning. Remember that only the writing on the lined pages will be scored.

The graders who score your writing will consider the organization of the piece and the supporting details. They will also consider grammar and sentence structure.

Next comes the writing situation. This part gives the background of the situation about which you are writing. It also explains the audience for the writing task. The instructions consist of three distinct paragraphs.

The first paragraph of the situation generally sets up the topic or the issue. This reflects a controversy based upon differences of opinion among people. This paragraph is approximately six sentences. Read this very carefully!

The second paragraph of the writing situation gives the purpose for writing and the audience for whom you are writing. This is two to three sentences.

The third paragraph is labeled "Directions for Writing."

These are the specific directions to follow in your writing. Read these carefully; most of the prompts ask that you write an essay, but it is also possible that you could be asked to write a letter. These directions remind you to support your position with reasons, examples, facts, and/or other evidence.

WRITING SITUATION

Numerous studies show that teenagers should start school later than 8 o'clock. The majority of these studies demonstrate that younger children are ready to begin their day early and are tired by midafternoon, and that teenagers are ready to begin their day midmorning and are not tired in the afternoon. The Board of Education has taken these studies into account and decided to change the hours of the high school day. The high school would begin at 9:30 and end at 4:30. This position has created controversy in the community.

Parents and students are worried about the effect a time change would have on after-school activities. Working parents sometimes need older children at home to help take care of siblings. Yet the scientific evidence seems to show that a later starting time would optimize learning. Your English teacher has asked you to write an essay explaining your position on this controversial issue.

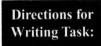

| Directions for Writing Task: | Write an essay supporting or opposing the change in the high school hours. Use facts, examples, and other evidence to support your point of view. |

WHAT ARE YOU BEING ASKED TO DO?

You are being asked to write a persuasive essay. This is formal expository writing, not creative writing. Use a standard writing structure, transitions, and formal English grammar.

The easiest structure to use may be the standard five-paragraph essay structure. Start with an introduction that states the issue, your opinion, and the premises (main ideas) that support that opinion. Each body paragraph uses one of these premises as a topic sentence and supports the idea with details and examples. The final, concluding paragraph reiterates your opinion (thesis) and summarizes your premises.

THINKING IT THROUGH

First, underline the parts of the writing situation that are most important. In the sample prompt you might underline
"The high school would begin at 9:30 and end at 4:30."
That is the basic piece of information with which you are working.

Now You Try It!

In the following writing situation <u>underline</u> the most important pieces of information:

WRITING SITUATION

A number of students in your school have presented a petition to the principal requesting that girls be permitted to try out for varsity boys' teams and that some interscholastic sports be open to both boys and girls on the same team. To support the request, the petition points out that some time ago, one of the best singles players on a New Jersey varsity tennis team was a girl. The petition states that varsity tennis should be coed as should varsity wrestling. The petition requests that your school follow the lead of some of the schools that have already taken tentative steps toward coed sports.

In order to think about this idea the most important piece of information is what the petition is asking. That is the sentence you should have underlined.

It is usually easiest to persuade the reader if you believe in what you are writing. Know what you think before beginning formal planning. Prewriting techniques can be useful in this case. There are a number of prewriting techniques that will help you think about the essay you are going to write.

FREEWRITING

For the writing situation in the prompt that follows, you are going to free-write for two minutes. Freewriting is just thinking on paper without formal sentence structure or grammar.

WRITING SITUATION

Numerous studies show that teenagers should start school later than 8 o'clock. The majority of these studies demonstrate that younger children are ready to begin their day early and are tired by midafternoon, and that teenagers are ready to begin their day midmorning and are not tired in the afternoon. The Board of Education has taken these studies into account and decided to change the hours of the high school day. The high school would begin at 9:30 and end at 4:30. This position has created controversy in the community. Parents and students are worried about the effect a time change would have on after-school activities. Working parents sometimes need older children at home to help take care of siblings. Yet the scientific evidence seems to show that a later starting time would optimize learning.

Now free-write about the topic for two minutes. (Time yourself!)

_____

_____

_____

_____

_____

_____

_____

_____

_____

_____

_____

_____

_____

_____

_____

_____

_____

_____

_____

_____

_____

_____

_____

_____

_____

_____

_____

_____

Go back and read what you have written. (This should take approximately one minute.) Underline anything that is interesting as you read.

Sample Free-Write

It would be nice to be able to sleep in the morning—I'm always tired during first period, usually the first two periods and I think it would be easier to concentrate if I was more awake . . . but I might have to stay up later at night because if I don't get finished until 4:30 and then have to go to practice I will not get home until 8:30 and once I eat I really won't start homework until 9:30 or 10—although sometimes I don't start homework until then anyway because I'm on line or playing video games—and I never get to eat dinner with my family now anyway so that wouldn't be a problem. I would get to see my little sister in the morning because she always is tired by the time I get in and she seems really wide awake in the morning—she's up before I am.

When the writer read over the free-write he decided that he could find many reasons to start school later and that was the opinion he would use in his writing. (Most freewriting looks more like "Net speak" than the sample.)

MAKING LISTS

Another method of thinking is to make fast lists:

For later hours

Tired in morning

Don't pay attention

Stay up late anyway

Work better later at night

During the weekend my job is from late afternoon until late at night—same hours

Against later hours

Sports would start late—other schools would be on a different schedule.

Transportation would be a problem.

Some kids wouldn't be able to work after school and they need to—would get out of school too late.

Some kids need to watch brothers and sisters while their parents work.

WEBBING

After this writer looked over the list, she decided there were better reasons to keep the current school hours. This is the position she presented in her essay.

For writers who are visual, webbing might be easiest:

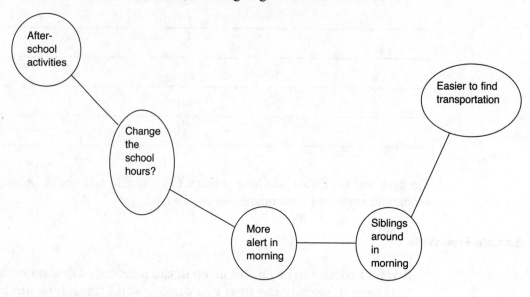

QUESTIONING

Some of us prefer to ask ourselves questions:

What would be the benefits to me if school started later?

_____

_____

_____

_____

What would be harder for me if school started later?

_____

_____

_____

_____

What benefits does the writing situation note?

_____

_____

_____

_____

What negatives does the writing situation note?

_____

_____

_____

_____

_____

Do the benefits outweigh the negatives? Why?

_____

_____

_____

_____

PREWRITING: TEN MINUTES THAT CAN MAKE A DIFFERENCE!

Know what you are going to say and the details to be used in support of your idea before beginning the actual process of writing. There is only time to write one draft and then edit and do minor revisions.

You do not have time to change your opinion once you have begun to write.

This makes prewriting more important than usual.

Methods of Organizing

Everyone has a favorite method of quickly organizing writing. Some of us prefer an informal outline. Some people prefer a flowchart. Some people just list ideas and then circle those that go together. Whatever method you use, practice it until it becomes second nature.

Method 1

INFORMAL OUTLINE

Introduction

1. Thesis statement
   a. Supporting idea 1
   b. Supporting idea 2
   c. Supporting idea 3

2. Body paragraph 1—supporting idea 1
   a. Reasons
   b. Example
   c. Example
   d. Transition

3. Body paragraph 2—supporting idea 2
   a. Reasons
   b. Example
   c. Reason or example

4. Body paragraph 3—supporting idea 3
   a. Reasons
   b. Example
   c. Reason or example

5. Conclusion
   a. Restatement of thesis

Method 2

A FLOWCHART

A flowchart looks something like this:

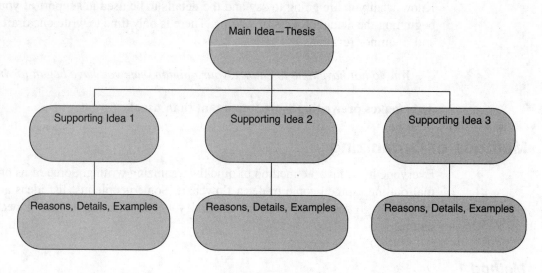

Thesis Statement

Supporting Idea 1	Supporting Idea 2	Supporting Idea 3
reasons	reasons	reasons
details	details	details
examples	examples	examples

Method 3

WEBBING

This is what a web looks like:

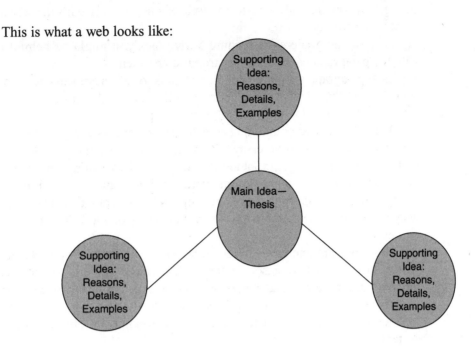

Writing the Thesis Statement

The thesis statement of a persuasive essay is different from a thesis statement for a paper. This thesis is a statement of opinion. You must be *for* or *against* an idea. Do not "sit on the fence." The argument can be strongly supported only if the thesis is decisive.

However, there are certain terms that should <u>not</u> be used in a thesis statement for a persuasive essay; they make it difficult to prove the point. Try to avoid the following:

all	every	none
never	always	
best	worst	

These words are so inclusive that if the reader can think of one contrasting point, you have lost your case.

Make the thesis statement clear; don't make it so long that the reader is lost. You may borrow the beginning of the thesis from the writing situation.

> *Example: Changing the hours for high school to 9:30 to 4:30 would not be beneficial to the majority of students.*

Or

> *Example: Changing the hours for high school to 9:30 to 4:30 would be beneficial to students.*

Do not do more work than necessary! Use the line in the text as the basis for the thesis and add your opinion.

Paragraph Organization

There are really only two ways to organize the paragraphs in this essay. Start with the strongest argument and work to the weaker one, or start with the weaker argument and work to the stronger one.

Because the graders are reading fairly quickly, it might be helpful to start the body with the paragraph containing the strongest argument.

Each paragraph should be coherent; that is to say, every sentence should logically add something to the one that came before and flow smoothly into the one that comes after it. Do not suddenly add a new idea to the paragraph.

Although there are numerous ways to arrange details in a paragraph, only two of them are useful for a persuasive essay. The topic sentence should be either the first or second sentence of each paragraph; other placement requires writing time that you do not have. You can then arrange the paragraph in order of importance, either from the most important detail to the least important detail or the opposite. Or arrange the paragraph in logical order where each sentence supports the topic sentence, using a different example and connecting reasons.

Most good arguments are based on research, but obviously this can not be done for this writing task. So stick to reason and example for basic support. Your job is to be certain that the relationship between sentences and between paragraphs is made clear to the reader.

There are two ways to help keep thoughts flowing from one sentence to the next. Practice these techniques. The first is to use pronouns to refer to words in the preceding sentence:

Cats make wonderful pets. They are easy to care for and they are inexpensive to maintain. (clear reference—they refers to cats)

You have to be careful that you have a <u>clear</u> pronoun reference.

Cats can be trained almost as easily as dogs. The tricks they do can impress many people. (unclear who they is)

The second way to keep thoughts flowing is to use "connectives" when the connection is not clear to the reader. The following is a list of the most useful connectives:

accordingly	hence
again	in addition
also	additionally
although	nevertheless
as a result	next
at the same time	on the contrary
simultaneously	conversely
beyond	otherwise
consequently	secondly
finally	secondly
first	second
for example	then
for instance	thus

Be aware of using transitions between paragraphs. The above connectives work well in most cases. The alternative is to use a word or phrase from the preceding paragraph in the topic sentence of the next paragraph or the first sentence of the next paragraph.

Supporting Your Ideas

These are the major ways to support an argument:

- Statistics
- Facts
- Evidence
- Expert Testimony
- Prediction
- Observation
- Comparison
- Experience
- Analogies

Several of these are not possible in this writing situation. For example, it is unlikely that you have memorized statistics that could be used. (No, you cannot make them up!) Rely on your own observation, experience, and analysis to produce most of the piece of writing.

After completing the prewriting steps, the analysis part is done. Now supply examples from experience and observation to support the ideas.

WRITING THE ESSAY

Once the essay is planned and the prewriting done, the majority of the thinking is finished.

Opening

The opening paragraph should start with an interesting sentence. Generally you can ask a rhetorical question or give an example. Several of the methods of developing an interesting opening are not possible in this type of testing; for example, it is unlikely that you happen to have a quotation memorized that fits the question. Although it is a good idea to start with an interesting sentence, it is not always necessary in test writing. Do NOT waste a lot of time trying to start the essay. If you can't think of anything, just start with your thesis. If there is time at the end of the testing period, you can go back and struggle with the first sentence. Be sure the thesis is clearly stated. It is better to be boring and clear than fascinating and muddy.

Each of the main reasons noted in your prewriting should be in the opening paragraph. Think of this paragraph as an outline of the most important points that will be made.

Body Paragraphs

The body paragraphs must have clear topic sentences that are linked to the thesis statement. The paragraph should include the benefits or disadvantages that go along with the topic sentence. Give at least one developed example of a benefit or a disadvantage. If you know any facts that support your argument, put them in. (Do not make up facts.)

Conclusion

The conclusion is the last thing the graders read. Wording and logic are important in this paragraph. Be certain that there are no contradictions, and make sure to restate the original thesis.

REVISING AND EDITING

Keep in mind that the readers understand that this is not a paper on which a student had hours to work. When you revise or edit, look for the obvious grammatical errors. First read for

- ✔ sentence fragments
- ✔ run-on sentences
- ✔ spelling
- ✔ punctuation
- ✔ capitalization
- ✔ transitions

Next, if time allows, read for variety in sentence structure. If the prewriting plan is followed, there is no need to worry about the structure and organization.

How Are You Scored?

This piece of writing is scored holistically. That means that there are two readers. Each person reads your piece and assigns it a number from 1 to 6 according to the New Jersey Registered Holistic Scoring Guide. The two numbers are added together to get a total score. The entire section is worth 0 to 12 points.

There are four possible reasons that you would get a 0 (nonscorable response):

1. FR—fragment
   (You did not write enough for the graders to score the piece.)
2. OT—off topic, off task
   (You did not respond to the question but wrote about something else. You wrote a short story, not a persuasive essay. You wrote a dialogue.)
3. NE—not English
   (You wrote the majority of the essay in a language other than English.)
4. WF—wrong format
   (The writing task folder is blank. You wrote a letter to Santa Claus.)

The graders are looking for the following:

1. There is a distinct opening and closing.
   (Each should be a paragraph—that makes it easy to see that you do have an opening and closing.)
2. Each supporting paragraph is clearly linked to your opinion and supports your opinion.
3. You have written about only one opinion. You did not change your mind halfway through the essay.
4. The ideas are not just thrown together but are logically placed to build your case.
5. You have used an analogy, simile, metaphor, or other rhetorical device that is considered a "compositional risk." You have demonstrated that you can control language.
6. All of your examples and details support your ideas and are effective in convincing the reader that you are right.
7. There are no errors in wording or sentence structure that "stop" the reader.
8. Sentence structure is varied enough that it is not boring and repetitive.
9. Spelling, capitalization, and punctuation are correct. (If you have spelled one word incorrectly, it is not a problem. If you have spelled one word incorrectly and repeat that word 15 times in the essay, it is a problem.)

The actual rubric is available at the back of this book <u>or</u> online at the New Jersey Department of Education Web Site, Standards and Assessment, Sample HSPA test.

PUTTING IT ALL TOGETHER: SAMPLE PERSUASIVE WRITING TASK QUESTIONS

Now it is your turn to try a prompt. It is important to note the time and take the full 60 minutes. Remember to think through the task (prewrite), plan, write, and read what you wrote.

WRITING SITUATION

Recently, there have been a number of fatal accidents caused by drivers who were under the influence of drugs. The legislature is looking at a proposal that the state pass a law requiring random drug testing of all drivers. Some people believe that this is a good idea and that it would significantly cut down on the number of accidents. They point to the DWI laws and their positive results as reason enough to enforce the same type of testing for drugs. Other people oppose this idea, believing that it would violate their civil rights and, potentially, give the police too much power.

Your local council has asked that each student write an essay either supporting or opposing state mandated, random drug testing of all drivers. The council members will read these essays to help them decide their position.

Directions for Writing:	Write your essay. Support your position with reasons, examples, facts, or other evidence. Persuade the reader to take your position seriously even if they do not agree with you.

PREWRITING/PLANNING

(Remember, this page would not be scored.)

WRITING

Now go back and check your work.
Highlight the thesis statement. Check off the following if the answer is yes.

_____ Does it make a statement that you think random drug testing should be mandated?

_____ Does it make a statement that random drug testing should NOT be mandated?

You should have a check mark next to one of the above. If not, your thesis is not tied directly to the question. Rewrite your thesis.

_____ Does the opening paragraph contain general reasons?

The first paragraph should give the reader the major ideas (reasons that are going to be developed in the remainder of the essay).

_____ Does the opening paragraph contain specific details or examples?
If this paragraph does contain specifics, other than as an interesting first sentence, then you need to get rid of them. Details and specifics are used in the body paragraphs.

HIGHLIGHT the topic sentences of each body paragraph.

_____ Does each topic sentence support the thesis?

_____ Does each paragraph discuss a different reason?

_____ Does each topic sentence make sense?

In each paragraph, number the details and examples.

_____ Are there enough details or examples to support the topic sentence? (One example will not make a case.)

_____ Does each detail or example have something to do with the topic sentence?

_____ Are the details and examples linked fluently? (Do they seem to go together well?)

Conclusion

_____ Does the conclusion state the same opinion that is in the thesis?

NOW, proofread for mechanics.
Sentence Structure

_____ Is the sentence structure varied? (You don't have the same pattern constantly.)

_____ There are no run-on sentences. (You don't have to take a breath before you finish the sentence.)

_____ There are no sentence fragments. (Each sentence is a complete thought.)

Mechanics

_____ Check punctuation.

_____ Check capitalization.

_____ Check for correct spelling, including homonyms.

WRITING SITUATION

Merchants in some towns offer discounts to honor students from the local high school. This has been a controversial policy. Some students and parents believe this is a wonderful incentive for students who excel through hard work. Other students and parents point out that people who have average grades but participate in other activities should also be rewarded. Is this a good policy?

The chamber of commerce has asked for written opinions from the citizens of the town. Chamber members will read them before their next meeting.

Directions for Writing:	Write an essay in which you explain why offering discounts to honor students is or is not a fair policy. Include specific reasons for your arguments and support your argument with details and examples.

PREWRITING/PLANNING

(Remember, this page would not be scored.)

WRITING

Now go back and check your work.

Highlight the thesis statement. Check off the following if the answer is yes:

_____ Does it make the statement that you think offering discounts to honor students is a good policy?

_____ Does it make the statement that offering discounts to honor students is NOT a good policy?

You should have a check mark next to one of the above. If you do not, the thesis is not tied directly to the question. If both are checked, you have not taken a position. Rewrite the thesis.

_____ Does the opening paragraph contain general reasons?

The first paragraph should give the reader the major ideas (reasons that are going to be developed in the remainder of the essay).

_____ Does the opening paragraph contain specific details or examples?

If this paragraph does contain specifics, other than as an interesting first sentence, then you need to get rid of them. Details and specifics are used in the body paragraphs.

HIGHLIGHT the topic sentences of each body paragraph.

_____ Does each topic sentence support the thesis?

_____ Does each paragraph discuss a different reason?

_____ Does each topic sentence make sense?

In each paragraph, number the details and examples.

_____ Are there enough details or examples to support the topic sentence? (One example will not make a case.)

_____ Does each detail or example have something to do with the topic sentence?

_____ Are the details and examples linked fluently? (Do they seem to go together well?)

Conclusion

_____ Does the conclusion state the same opinion that is in the thesis?

NOW, proofread for mechanics.

Sentence Structure

_____ Is the sentence structure varied? (You don't have the same pattern constantly.)

_____ There are no run-on sentences. (You don't have to take a breath before you finish the sentence.)

_____ There are no sentence fragments. (Each sentence is a complete thought.)

Mechanics

_____ Check punctuation.

_____ Check capitalization.

_____ Check for correct spelling, including homonyms.

ADDITIONAL PRACTICE PERSUASIVE WRITING PROMPTS

Directions: In this part of the test you will complete a writing task which gives you an opportunity to demonstrate how well you can organize and express your ideas in written text. You have been provided with a Writer's Checklist that lists important points to remember while you write; the graders will consider these points as they read and score your writing.

You will have 60 minutes to complete this task. Take the first few minutes to think and plan what you want to write about. You may use the Prewriting/Planning space in your test booklet, but nothing that you write in this space will be scored. Keep both your audience and the purpose you are writing in mind. Try to keep your writing clear and well organized.

You must use a No. 2 pencil to write. You may either write or print your final copy. You may not use any reference materials other than the Writer's Checklist during the test. When you are finished writing read over your work. Revise and edit to improve what you have written.

WRITING SITUATION

Over the past few years, a large development company has been trying to get permission to build a large mall on the last few wooded acres in your town. Some people feel that the mall will bring in many new jobs for the residents of the town, which is greatly needed in the current economy. Others feel that building the mall will change the country feel of the town and destroy the homes of the few remaining animals in the woods.

The mayor and town council have asked town residents to express their feelings at the next town meeting. The mayor will listen to residents' opinions in order to help them decide whether or not to allow the developer to build this mall.

Directions for Writing: Write a statement/speech that you will deliver at the next town council meeting explaining your position on the mall development project. Support your position with reasons, examples, facts, or other evidence.

PREWRITING/PLANNING

(Remember, this page would not be scored.)

WRITING

Directions:

In this part of the test you will complete a writing task which gives you an opportunity to demonstrate how well you can organize and express your ideas in written text. You have been provided with a Writer's Checklist that lists important points to remember while you write; the graders will consider these points as they read and score your writing.

You will have 60 minutes to complete this task. Take the first few minutes to think and plan what you want to write about. You may use the Prewriting/Planning space in your test booklet, but nothing that you write in this space will be scored. Keep both your audience and the purpose you are writing in mind. Try to keep your writing clear and well organized.

You must use a No. 2 pencil to write. You may either write or print your final copy. You may not use any reference materials other than the Writer's Checklist during the test. When you are finished writing read over your work. Revise and edit to improve what you have written.

WRITING SITUATION

Your high school has had the same mascot for years. It is a recognizable figure at every sporting event and it appears on school jackets, sweatpants, and on a crest in the front lobby of the school. Recently, a large manufacturer has offered to buy new uniforms for all the sports teams and totally renovate the gymnasium if they can design a new mascot that will advertise their product. The school administration has decided to leave the decision up to the students. Some students want to keep the traditional mascot and old uniforms, while others say that a new gym and new uniforms are more important than the mascot.

The Student Council wants to find out how students feel about this issue. They have asked that you write a letter to the editor of the school paper explaining your position on changing the mascot.

Directions for Writing:

Write a letter to the editor explaining your point of view. Do you wish to accept the new gym, uniforms, and a new mascot, or do you feel that the traditional mascot should be maintained? Support your position with reasons, examples, facts, or other evidence.

PREWRITING/PLANNING

(Remember, this page would not be scored.)

WRITING

Chapter 5 | Reading and Responding to a Persuasive Passage

OVERVIEW: WHAT IS A "PERSUASIVE PASSAGE" AND HOW WILL IT LOOK?

A persuasive text is defined as text in which the writer attempts to sway the reader to a specific point of view. The passages you will be asked to read are selected from previously published works such as essays, speeches, book or movie reviews, editorials, political literature, or other persuasive writings. The length of these passages is between 1,000 and 1,600 words and, similar to the narrative passages, may be excerpts or full works. The following is a list of the common elements that may be found in the persuasive texts chosen for this assessment:

- Topics will be age-appropriate.
- Passages will have a clear theme or central idea.
- Passages will use facts and opinions to support the central idea.
- Passages will use persuasive techniques such as propaganda, connotative and figurative language, and rhetorical devices.
- Passages will use vocabulary for which adequate context clues are provided.

The remainder of this chapter discusses these key elements of persuasive writing and gives you the opportunity to practice important strategies so that you can become a careful, thoughtful reader and writer.

Each persuasive passage has a brief introduction in italics before the title and author of the selection. This introduction can offer some very important information and should be read! It may explain what the selection is about, tell whether it is an excerpt or a complete work, and may indicate the author's purpose for writing. These few sentences will help prepare you for what you are about to read and can be very helpful in answering some of the multiple-choice questions afterward. If there is a title, take note of that before beginning to read.

Immediately after the persuasive passage are ten multiple-choice questions and two open-ended questions. These will be explained fully in the rest of this chapter. You will have a total of 45 minutes to complete the reading and answer the multiple-choice and open-ended questions. Answer the multiple-choice questions by filling in the correct circle on your answer sheet; you will be given lined space in the answer booklet to answer the open-ended questions.

The directions for this part of the HSPA in Language Arts Literacy will look like this:

Directions: In this part of the test, you will read a persuasive passage and then respond to the multiple-choice and open-ended questions that follow it. You may look back at the passage and make notes in your test booklet, if you like.

You will have 45 minutes for this part of the test. If you finish this part before the time is called, close your test booklet and wait quietly until you receive further instructions.

The next page will say "Reading: Persuasive Text." The directions will be repeated:

Directions for questions 1–10:	Read the passage and record your answers to the multiple-choice questions in your answer folder. Just as in the narrative passage reading, you will first read one or more "introductory" sentences. The reading selection will be organized in two columns and indicate to "go on to the next page" until the passage is finished.

WHAT ARE YOU BEING ASKED TO DO?

In Chapter 3 of this book, specific skills of careful, active, and engaged readers were discussed. These same skills will be assessed for this portion of the HSPA through your answers on the multiple-choice and open-ended questions. Take a moment to reread these important skills:

1. Recognizing central ideas and/or themes
2. Recognizing supporting details
3. Extrapolation of information/following directions
4. Paraphrasing/retelling
5. Recognizing how a text is organized
6. Recognizing the author's intended purpose
7. Questioning
8. Making predictions of tentative meanings
9. Forming opinions
10. Drawing conclusions
11. Interpretation of textual conventions and literary elements

These skills were discussed at length in Chapter 3. You may want to take a few moments to review what is said about these skills there. The sample persuasive reading passage at the end of this chapter indicates the specific skill or skills associated with each multiple-choice question. This will help you know which strategies may require further practice to succeed on the HSPA.

READING STRATEGIES FOR PERSUASIVE PASSAGES

There will be a brief introduction to the persuasive passage you are asked to read. Often, this introduction will summarize the focus of the persuasive piece. It might also provide the reader with the purpose of the writing or the attitude of the author. Make certain to read the introduction carefully!

Persuasive passages can easily be broken down into their component parts. The thesis is the major idea the writer is trying to convey. Each thesis statement will be supported by minor ideas or reasons. These reasons will, generally, be the topic sentences of the body paragraphs. **As you are reading highlight both the thesis statement and the topic sentences of paragraphs**; this will let you quickly find the argument and see the structure of the argument with which the writer is dealing.

Each paragraph will be supported by statistics, facts, examples, or illustrations. As you read, consider the method that the writer has chosen to organize his or her piece. There are four major methods that writers might use to organize a persuasive essay: order of increasing importance, order of decreasing importance, chronological order, and comparison and contrast. Take note of how the piece develops as you read each selection.

It is important to think about the author's purpose for writing. You can often determine the purpose by combining the thesis with the tone of the piece. For example, an author's thesis is that college students living in dorms should not keep pets. Both the word choice and the choice of examples create the tone. In this case, you will see that the purpose (as reflected in the tone) is to make the reader aware of this situation. If the writer had wanted the reader to respond immediately and actively to this problem, the examples given would be more graphic and more horrifying.

The ending paragraph or paragraphs in a persuasive piece of writing is usually a call for action; the writer wants the reader to actively respond to the focus of the piece.

MULTIPLE-CHOICE QUESTIONS: STRATEGIES FOR PERSUASIVE PASSAGES

The same strategies discussed in Chapter 3 regarding the reading of narrative passages are applicable to the persuasive multiple-choice questions and open-ended questions. It might be helpful to take a few minutes to review these strategies before continuing.

Every multiple-choice question is worth one point. You are not penalized for getting an answer wrong, so it pays to guess. If time is remaining at the end of the test, you can always go back to a question.

The kinds of questions asked regarding the persuasive passage will differ in some ways from the questions you answered for the narrative passages. There will most probably be questions about a "central idea" or the purpose of the passage, questions about the author's point of view, and questions that highlight the intended audience for the selection. There may also be a number of vocabulary questions in this section, because the connotation of words is most important in persuasive writing.

Additionally, you will be asked questions requiring you to find and understand supporting details, the method of organization, and the author's point of view. You will have to make inferences based on the reading. You are not, necessarily, being asked your own opinion on the subject.

OPEN-ENDED QUESTIONS: STRATEGIES FOR ANSWERING THESE QUESTIONS

Once again, the strategies for answering open-ended questions as discussed in Chapter 3 for narrative passages are equally appropriate for persuasive selections.

Each open-ended question on the HSPA consists of a statement followed by two related questions. These questions are related in a variety of ways. Sometimes one asks you to formulate an opinion and the other asks that you apply that opinion to a specific example. Sometimes the second question simply asks the writer to elaborate on the first response. Often you are asked something specific about the text in the first question and then asked to make an inference in the second question. Each of these questions is preceded by a bullet. After each open-ended question there will be a reminder to "use information from the text to support your response."

Open-ended questions are meant to be harder than the multiple-choice questions. There is no one right answer to these questions, but the grader wants to see that you are a thoughtful, careful reader who is able to connect with the reading selection.

HOW WILL YOU BE SCORED?

The scoring rubric for the open-ended questions is based on a 4-point scale. That means that a student can score from 0 to 4 on these questions. There are four open-ended questions on the Language Arts HSPA: two after the narrative reading passage and multiple-choice questions, and two after the persuasive reading passage and multiple-choice questions. This means that for ALL of the open-ended questions you could score a possible total of 16 points.

Two readers will read each answer, and the score will be an average of the points they award your response. A 0-point response means that what has been written is off topic (the question has not been answered). A 4-point response means that you have understood the task, completed all portions of the open-ended question (the bulleted items), and given a thoughtful answer that connects with and uses the text. The rubric itself will look something like this:

Points	Criteria
4	The writer has understood the task, completed all bulleted requirements, and written a thoughtful, complete answer that is supported by the text material and may even extend the ideas in the text (goes beyond #3).
3	The writer has understood the task, completed all bulleted requirements, and written a response using ideas/information from the text for support.
2	The writer may have completed all of the bulleted requirements but shows only a partial understanding of the task and uses the text minimally so that his/her ideas are not supported very well.
1	The writer does not seem to understand the task, does not complete all of the bulleted requirements, and uses little if any of the text.
0	This response is off topic (has not attempted to answer the question).

Based upon this scoring rubric, you can see why the authors of this book keep reminding you to answer each and every portion of the open-ended response and to use the text to support your answer. Notice that this is the only way to receive a high score on the open-ended questions. You will be graded only on the criteria that is in the rubric: that means that spelling, mechanics, organization, and good opening and strong closing sentences are not as important as the criteria listed above. Traditional mechanics will not count against you as you write the open-ended questions. However, please realize that a strong opening, relevant supporting details, organization, and well-constructed sentences will make the response more readable and give the grader a favorable impression.

What follows are the terms and techniques used in persuasive writing. As you read the persuasive selections and work through the sample exercises, be aware of the meanings of these words.

TERMS AND TECHNIQUES USED IN PERSUASIVE WRITING

Comparison	The similarities between two things or ideas.
	Example: The SAT and the HSPA contain similar vocabulary-in-context questions.
Contrast	Two opposing ideas.
	Example: Parents believe in a curfew for students, although most students consider a curfew unnecessary.
Elaboration	The addition of numerous details.
	Example: Her new blouse had frilly sleeves, a scoop neckline, and fringe on the bottom.
Exaggerated statements	Statements that have a basis in truth but have been distorted by emotion.
	Example: If I get a D on this test, my parents will disown me!
Fact	A fact is something that can be verified (proven).
	Example: Most students would rather be doing something else right now!
Inference	To use facts as a basis for speculation or judgment.
	Example: Because he studied for hours, he assumed he would do well on the test.
Opinion	An opinion cannot be verified; it is a statement of belief.
	Example: I think Sunday will be sunny.
Point of view	The perspective of the author.
Propaganda	Carefully selected information designed with the intent of having you believe a specific view.
Relevant examples	Examples that directly support an idea.
	Example: Dogs make wonderful pets because they are loyal. One collie walked fifty miles to return to his home.
Rhetorical questions	Questions asked for effect, but not with the expectation of an answer.
	Example: Don't you agree?
Sarcasm	Words that are personal, jeering, and intended to hurt.
	Example: Keep eating and you'll never fit through the doorway!
Selection of details	An author chooses to emphasize some details and leave out other details; this purposely biases the readers' opinion.
Sequence	The order of events, ideas, or actions.

PUTTING IT ALL TOGETHER
SAMPLE PERSUASIVE PASSAGE: MULTIPLE-CHOICE AND
OPEN-ENDED QUESTIONS

Read the following selection and answer the multiple-choice and open-ended questions that follow.

Use the strategies learned in this chapter as you read the selection. Check the answers using the answer key later in this chapter. Take note of the skills that seem to be your weakest and review that section.

Reading: Persuasive Passage

Rules and regulations don't always seem very fair, but they are usually created for extremely good reasons. Kymberlie Matthews-Adams writes of the horrors that can occur when this particular rule is broken.

Breaking the No-Pet Rule
By Kymberlie Matthews-Adams

1   Most colleges maintain a no-pet rule essentially stating that "for reasons of health, sanitation and noise concerns, pets of any type may not be kept in the residential areas with the exception of fish in proper aquarium facilities (capacity of 10 gallons or less)." Presumably students accept the regulation when they sign their housing contract. They also receive a booklet outlining residence hall policies and the rationale for those policies when they initially move in.

2   Yet it is a guarantee that a number of students violate this simple residence hall policy every year by harboring unauthorized and illegal companion animals in their dorm rooms and apartments.

3   Perhaps the violations stem from the simple pleasure of human/animal interactions. The benefits of human/animal relationships are limitless. Companion animals are found to relieve stress, provide companionship, encourage social interaction, and allow a sense of family, reassurances many students seek.

4   However, pet-policy violators cause thousands of animals each year to suffer from malnutrition, disease, abuse, neglect, and eventually abandonment. Dogs, cats, ducks, ferrets, birds, sugar gliders, hedgehogs, mice, rats, chinchillas, lemurs, snakes, squirrels, and hamsters are just a few of the animals that pine for a way out. (See "Pocket Pets," Spring 2001.)

5   Illegally harbored "dorm pets" often spend hours, even days, locked in closets, boxes, or secured under the bed while students are in class, out socializing, or away for the weekend. Isolated in darkness, dorm pets are sentenced to a stressful, constrained existence with little or no chance to behave naturally. As a result they exhibit stereotypic behaviors, such as pacing, hiding, biting, often becoming a threat to the safety of students.

6   On a limited budget, most students cannot afford their own lifestyles let alone caring for a companion animal. Dorm-pet violators can rarely provide suitable veterinary care or the proper dietary food required for their animal. Dorm pets are fed table scraps, junk food, or any available items including garbage. A poor diet often leads to malnutrition and numerable related diseases. Many dorm-pets also suffer from untreated broken limbs, cuts, sores, and bruises.

7   When winter recess or summer break liberates the student population, many dorm-pet violators find themselves inconvenienced. Mom and Dad won't be pleased to see them walking into the house with an unexpected guest of a different phylum. Many students deem that they have no option but to abandon their seasonal pals. "Before people adopt their pets, they really need to think about what they're going to do with them as Christmas comes, when the summer comes and when they graduate," says Jennifer Gentry, president and founder of Aggies Animal Welfare and Rights Ethics (AWARE), Bryon College.

8   Days, weeks go by before the college janitorial staff begins cleaning the dorm rooms. Among discarded notebooks, soiled sheets, ripped posters, and heaps of dirty clothes the remains of a lizard is found. An emaciated dog cowers in the closet only to be taken away by animal control. Tanks of algae and rotting fish decorate a barren desk. And under the bed curls the body of a cat that died of dehydration four days ago. "It is so sad, you never

know what you will find," says Ira Lang, janitor at the State University of New York. "We count on finding animals left behind. We just don't know what to do with the ones still alive. I have four cats that I rescued from here."

9   Other dorm pets are released into the wild to fend for themselves. Not neutered or spayed, feral animals begin to breed. Overpopulated colonies are not new to campus towns. The animal shelter soon becomes the residence for many pets abandoned by students who took everything home but them. Concerned citizens and landlords will walk through the animal shelter doors and present the receptionist with a "pet" which, it seems, was too much a bother to take home. What once was a novel idea—a sugar glider for a mascot, a dog for show and tell—turns into a calamity.

10   Although humane societies, animal control, and certain university staff are becoming aware of the increasing problem with dorm pets, no conclusive data are available. Without statistical evidence it is difficult to surmise the extent of the problem.

11   We do know that most unwanted dorm pets will not find another home. In fact their chances of dying from disease, starvation, or under the wheels of an automobile are much greater.

12   "Neglect or abandonment of a companion animal is against the law in most states," says API Government Affairs Coordinator Nicole Paquette, "variously punishable by jail time, steep fines, and psychological counseling."

13   Unwanted dorm pets are often dumped or abandoned outside. There, they risk disease, injury, and starvation. "Outdoor cats, for instance, live an average of 3–5 years, compared to 15–18 years for an indoor cat," says veterinarian and API Companion Animal Coordinator Jean Hofve. Abandoned animals may be picked up for quick sale to research labs, biological supply companies, or dog fighters looking for cheap live "bait." Because students rarely have the money to spay or neuter dorm pets, the animals that do somehow survive will contribute more litters to the terrible overpopulation problem that sends more than eight million unwanted dogs and cats to their deaths in shelters every year.

14   There is an absolute lack of regulation when it comes to housing animals in dorm rooms. Insufficient penalties make the market for concealing dorm-pets much more appealing to students. Discovered pet policy usually means a warning from the Department of Housing for the first violation. When a student blatantly violates the policy for a second time he or she can have their case heard by either a staff member or a school judicial board. That still may not be enough. Barbara Keionig, founder of Home for All Animals (HAA), a small sanctuary that provides homes for strays, stated that "Violators are spoiled and immature. They should be forced to volunteer at an animal shelter to see what life is like for abandoned animals."

15   An article in *The Orion*, the college paper at California State University of Chico, tells how two former students decided the fate of their cat Hooter, who became an abandoned, starving alley cat. "Hooter's owners never took care of him," said Robert Pence, a resident at the campus apartment complex where Hooter's owners used to live. "I could always hear Hooter whining for food. His owners tried to get rid of him by dropping him off the side of the road somewhere but the cat came back." Pence said that he didn't think Hooter ever saw a veterinarian, because the cat had sores all over his body and was practically a skeleton. "Honestly I think they were abusive to Hooter," Pence said. "I remember hearing a couple stories about Hooter. One time they threw him in the freezer, and they used to lower him up and down a two-store balcony. They used to blow marijuana in his face." Hooter did stay in the apartment occasionally when he was a kitten, but he was kicked outside when his owners became angry with him for not using the litter box they only occasionally changed, Pence said.

16   The spring semester ended, and summertime came, which was good for Hooter since he had spent many cold nights outside. However, Hooter was left to fend for himself. "Everyone who lives here can find Hooter either under a car or on top of its hood," Pence said.

17   Unfortunately, Hooter's story is not so farfetched when college towns are notorious for the feral cat colonies caused by students abandoning their four-footed college "buddies." Until students learn that they are responsible for the lives they bring with them, Hooter's tragic story will remain typical of what the average dorm pet can expect.

From <u>Animal Issues</u>. Volume 32 Number 3, Fall 2001
Permission to reprint by the Animal Protection Institute.

Reading: Items for "Breaking the No-Pet Rule"

MULTIPLE-CHOICE QUESTIONS

1 Which of the following BEST expresses the central idea of this article?
  A The benefits of human/animal relationships are worth the risks.
  B Students living in dorms break many rules and should be punished.
  C Dorm pets can become a threat to the safety of students.
  D It is illegal, as well as cruel, to house a pet in a restricted housing situation.

2 In paragraph 2, the word *harboring* means
  A hiding
  B feeding
  C training
  D abusing

3 Paragraph 14 supports which of the following statements?
  A Much stronger penalties must be enforced if this practice is to be stopped.
  B Students need to be engaged in part-time jobs.
  C Abandoned animals are not easily adopted.
  D Dorm rooms are no place to house pets.

4 The statement "When winter recess or summer break liberates the student population, many dorm-pet violators find themselves inconvenienced" is an example of which of the following?
  A Exaggeration
  B Contrast
  C Understatement
  D Propaganda

5 Who would most likely use this article to support their position?
  A College students brought up on dorm violations
  B Parents and teachers
  C Animal rights activists
  D Dorm custodians

6 Why does the author use the story of Hooter?
  A She feels bad that the cat had to suffer.
  B Hooter serves to illustrate the main point of the essay.
  C She hopes a reader will adopt Hooter.
  D Hooter personalizes the story for the author.

7 According to the author, all of the following are reasons that counter her main premise with the exception of
  A companion animals relieve stress.
  B companion animals encourage social interaction.
  C companion animals give students a warm sense of family.
  D companion animals learn to adapt to any environment.

8 In paragraph 4, the word *pine* means
  A prays
  B digs
  C searches
  D yearns

9 Based on this article, which of the following would the author be most likely to support?
  A Rules making it legal to keep dorm pets.
  B Animal shelters in every college community.
  C Stronger enforcement of regulations by college officials.
  D Parental acceptance of dorm pets.

10 According to the author of this article, "suitable veterinary care" would include all of the following EXCEPT
  A obedience training.
  B inoculations against disease.
  C proper guidance on pet diet.
  D care for cuts, sores, bruises, and broken bones.

Directions for questions 11 and 12:	Write your response in the space provided in the answer folder. DO NOT WRITE ANY RESPONSES IN THE TEST BOOKLET.

11 In paragraph 14, the author says, "Insufficient penalties make the market for concealing dorm-pets much more appealing to students."
  • Imagine that you are serving as a student representative to the university's department of housing. What recommendations would you make regarding punishing students who break the no-pet rule?
  • What advice might you give freshmen when they move into a dorm?

Use information from the article to support your response.

_____

_____

_____

_____

_____

_____

_____

_____

_____

_____

_____

_____

_____

_____

_____

_____

_____

_____

_____

_____

_____

_____

_____

_____

_____

_____

_____

_____

_____

_____

_____

_____

_____

_____

_____

_____

_____

_____

_____

12 Imagine that you are living in a college dorm and that the students in the room next door are illegally housing an animal.
  • Give two arguments you might use to persuade your neighbors to return the pet.
  • How would you create interest in this growing problem?

Use information from the article to support your response.

_____

_____

_____

_____

_____

_____

_____

_____

_____

_____

Answer Key for Multiple-Choice Items for "Breaking the No-Pet Rule"

1. **D**	Skill #1	Recognition of central idea or theme
2. **A**	Skill #8	Prediction of tentative meanings
3. **A**	Skill #2	Recognition of supporting details
4. **C**	Skill #11	Interpretation of textual conventions and literary elements
5. **C**	Skill #6	Recognition for a purpose for reading
6. **B**	Skill #11	Interpretation of textual conventions and literary elements
7. **D**	Skill #3	Extrapolation of information
8. **D**	Skill #8	Prediction of tentative meanings
9. **C**	Skill #10	Drawing conclusions
10. **A**	Skill #2	Recognition of supporting details

OPEN-ENDED RESPONSE COMMENTS:

Use the open-ended rubric to correct your answers to questions 11 and 12. Make certain each part of the question has been answered and that you have used specific information from the text to support the answers.

11. Your answer must contain specific recommendations to solve this problem. Some of these might include dorm inspections, monetary penalties, expulsion, being banned from campus housing, or being banned from campus sports and activities. Or you might come up with your own, original recommendation.

   The second portion of this question should focus on specific advice you would tell a new student. This might include the consequences for the pet, the consequences for the student, or an explanation of the rules of the dormitory. Make sure to use information from the text to support your recommendations.

12. Make certain to give two arguments in your answer. These might include the facts that the pet is in psychological danger, the pet is not well fed, the pet needs human companionship, neglect of an animal is against the law, or any of the other arguments that are given in the text.

   For the second portion of this question, you might propose the formation of a campus organization, the writing of a newsletter, writing letters to editors of the local newspapers, or contact with local TV stations. Perhaps you might have original ideas as to how this could be accomplished. Make certain to use textual information to support the response.

Reading: Persuasive Passage

Water is the most important resource on our planet. We would not exist without it! The following is a speech given by Mr. Klaus Toepfer, Executive Director of the United Nations Environment Program, on World Water Day, March 22, 2002. (This selection is reprinted by permission of the United Nations Environment Program.)

Nairobi, 21 March 2002—The Millennium Declaration, adopted by Head of States, set for the world the following goals:

1   —To halve, by the year 2015, the proportion of the world's people whose income is less than one dollar a day, and the proportion of people who suffer from hunger;

2   —And, by the same date, to halve the proportion of people who are unable to reach or to afford safe drinking water.

3   In the light of this commitment, the theme of World Water Day in 2002, "Water for Development," is particularly appropriate. Without adequate clean water, there can be no escape from poverty. Water is the basis for good health and food production. This year, water pollution, poor sanitation and water shortages will kill over 12 million people. Millions more are in bad health and trapped in poverty, much of their energy and time wasted in the quest for clean water.

4   Seventy-five percent of water is used for agriculture. Crop failure due to lack of water, or too much water, can mean starvation for many.

5   Mankind is always at the mercy of water for survival and development. Water's almost sacred status, is recognized the world over. The Koran mentions that all life originated from water, and that man himself is created of water. Water's power to destroy is well known. In the Bible, floods and drought were punishments sent from God. In Judaism, water is important for ritual purification. The Incas believed that Lake Titicaca was the center of the original world, and water was the essential factor in the stability and prosperity of the Mayan peoples. The "sacred waters" of the Hindus erase caste distinctions. We too, should use water to restore equity.

6   Water is vital to economic development. We must recognize the true dimension of the challenge we face. The challenge of ensuring sustainable water on demand and use, and the supply of water to all. Appropriate action is required to meet this challenge.

7   There is a need for investment in water services and water conservation. Water resources must be developed and managed efficiently. Where appropriate, high-tech solutions for water conservation and recycling, such as those developed by UNEP's IETC should be implemented. Awareness at every level must be increased. If there is awareness, least-cost (often simple) solutions for sustainable water conservation such as roof rainwater collection, recycling and reuse, can also be put into practice.

8   Due attention should be given to the problem of trans-boundary waters. The development of legal frameworks for the equitable sharing of water resources is key to peace and stability, without which there can be no development.

9   Water-pricing needs to be revised to reflect the true cost of the resource, taking account of the economic, social, and environmental value of water. Such a policy will encourage more efficient use, and discourage waste. Pricing policy should of course take account of the limited finances of the poor. At present the poorest pay most for clean water, both in monetary terms, and in terms of the burden to their health. The problem is particularly acute in urban areas. Working with Habitat, through the project "Water for African Cities," UNEP is acting to tackle the urban water crisis in African cities. Water should be made available and affordable for all.

10   This year let us use "World Water Day" to open the eyes of the world to the lack of water for development, and the reasons behind this problem. World Water Day should mark the beginning of a new era of cooperation between the rich and the poor, in an attempt to provide clean water to those who have none, or very little.

11   We should make every effort to give a new perspective to the mil. trudging great distances to fetch water. We have to give new hope to the chi. and dying from water related diseases.

12   Let us make "World Water Day" more than a date in the calendar. Let this of action to meet the goals of the Millennium Declaration. Action, which we can . later this year, at the World Summit on Sustainable Development, in Johannesbur. Africa.

13   If we agreed with the words of Mahbub al Haq, "Sustainable development is a ᵩ tion of quality of life for the rich countries but it is a question of life for the pᵥ countries," I believe we have no choice but to act together responsibly to ensure water fᵤ all, for a better future.

Source: UNEP Information Note 2002/6, 22 March 2002

Reading: Items for World Water Day Speech

MULTIPLE-CHOICE QUESTIONS

1 How does the speaker build his argument in this piece?
  A Moves from a specific premise to general information.
  B Moves from the specific need to a call for action.
  C Moves from statistics to the premise.
  D Develops the speech from a historical perspective.

2 The speaker would agree with all of the following EXCEPT
  A clean adequate water is a start to escaping poverty.
  B drought and dirty water supplies kill millions of people each year.
  C clean water will create inequities among countries.
  D countries must allocate money to improve world water resources.

3 In paragraph 8, the word *trans-boundary* is used to describe
  A the problem of water spillage.
  B the legal boundaries for water regulation.
  C the borders of neighboring countries.
  D the issues of peace and stability.

4 The speaker says, "At present the poorest pay most for clean water, both in monetary terms, and in terms of the burden to their health." By this he means
  A poor people with limited resources can't afford clean water and are at risk of getting sick from unsanitary water.
  B poor people are charged extra tax on water and can't afford medical help.
  C poor people believe water is their most important resource and are willing to pay more for it.
  D poor people work long hours to pay for their water and therefore put their health at risk.

5 In the context of the quote, the word *sustainable* (paragraph 6) means
  A equitable
  B continued
  C enforceable
  D maintainable

6 The purpose of this speech is most likely
  A to entertain.
  B to celebrate the completion of "Water for Development."
  C to let U.N. representatives know about the Millennium Declaration.
  D To move world countries to action regarding issues of water conservation.

7 In paragraph 5, why does the speaker use examples from so many diverse cultures?
  A The more examples he uses, the stronger his case.
  B He wants to illustrate that water needs are universal.
  C He wants to appeal to all the people mentioned in the paragraph.
  D He wants the world to believe that water is sacred.

8 By the end of the speech, if it is successful, Mr. Toepfer hopes that
  A the world will celebrate World Water Day.
  B people will attend the World Summit on Sustainable Development.
  C countries will create task forces to help people reach and afford safe drinking water.
  D the world will discover a way to end droughts.

9 In paragraph 9, the speaker says, "The problem is particularly acute in urban areas." In this context, *acute* means
  A important
  B noticeable
  C obvious
  D severe

10 Which of the following quotations BEST supports the main idea of this speech?
  A "Water is the basis for good health and food production."
  B "Seventy-five percent of water is used for agriculture."
  C "Pricing policy should of course take account of the limited finances of the poor."
  D "Let this be the start of action to meet the goals of the Millennium Declaration."

Directions for questions 11 and 12:	Write your response in the space provided in the answer folder. DO NOT WRITE ANY RESPONSES IN THE TEST BOOKLET.

11 The speaker suggests that without "adequate clean water" the poor cannot escape from poverty.
  • Explain what you think the author means by this statement.
  • Explain how your life would be different if you did not have access to enough sanitary water.

Use information from the speech to support your response.

_____

_____

_____

_____

_____

_____

_____

_____

_____

_____

_____

_____

12 In discussing the issues of water services and water conservation, the speaker proposes a number of possible solutions to the problem.
- Which proposed solution do you see as the one most likely to be accepted by world countries?
- What solution might you propose in your own community to save water resources?

Use information from the speech to support your response.

_____

_____

_____

_____

_____

_____

_____

_____

_____

Answer Key for World Water Day Speech

1. **B**
2. **C**
3. **C**
4. **A**
5. **D**
6. **D**
7. **B**
8. **C**
9. **D**
10. **D**

Use the open-ended rubric to grade your answers to questions 11 and 12. Make certain that you have answered each part of the question and used specific information and quotes from the reading.

Chapter 6 | **Revising and Editing**

OVERVIEW: HOW WILL IT LOOK?

The revising and editing section was field tested in 2002; it may or may not be part of the HSPA you take. We are proceeding on the assumption that you may be taking this section.

The Revise/Edit sections of the HSPA will begin, as do the other sections, with a set of directions in a box on a separate page. It will explain that the task is to revise/edit another student's essay. That essay will be reprinted in the answer book, and the test materials will contain a Revising/Editing Guide to help with the kinds of editing changes you should be making. The answer folder will provide lined space to use.

You will be given the writing prompt on which the piece was based, so that you have an understanding of the purpose of the essay. You will also be given an indication of the audience for the piece.

You will have approximately 30 minutes to complete this task.

WHAT ARE YOU BEING ASKED TO DO?

This section will contain an essay, editorial, or other piece of student writing and ask that you change it to improve clarity, and to develop the ideas that are already in the writing. You will also be asked to edit the writing so that it is mechanically correct.

Although the directions may say that you are not required to rewrite the essay on the two lined pieces of paper in your answer book, rewriting the edited/revised work is probably the easiest approach.

WHAT ARE YOU <u>NOT</u> BEING ASKED TO DO?

You are <u>not</u> being asked to write a new essay on the topic.

You are <u>not</u> being asked to add additional information to the piece.

You are <u>not</u> changing the text to express your personal opinion.

As described above, this writing task will first give the writing situation. This basically defines the purpose of the piece. The writing situation language will be similar to the prompt given in the persuasive and picture writing tasks.

The introduction to this writing task will look like this:

Many schools are considering mandating school uniforms. This is a controversial issue in many school districts and has been a subject of serious debate.

The following is the first draft of an editorial that a student wrote for the local paper about this issue. Read this draft and think about how to improve the meaning and the clarity of the text. Then make your revision.

Before we go on, let's look at the phrase "improve the meaning and clarity of the text."

There are four areas to which you have to pay attention:

Content/Organization

- Opening and closing (introduction and conclusion)
- Development of key ideas (paragraph coherence)
- Logical progression of ideas (structure)
- Supporting details (do they exist?)
- Transitions (between paragraphs)

Sentence Construction

- Correct sentence structure (no run-ons, no sentence fragments, and correct syntax)
- Varied sentence structure (changes in sentence patterns)
- Correct subordination/coordination (the logic of the sentence works)

Usage

- Correct verb tenses
- Subject/verb agreement
- Pronoun usage and agreement
- Word choice

Mechanics

- Spelling (especially homonyms)
- Capitalization
- Punctuation

These are the areas that the graders have on the rubric. Ideally, they are looking for the following:

Content/Organization

- Consistent attention to opening and closing. (Have a solid introduction and a good conclusion.)
- Single, distinct focus. (Everything in the piece supports the main point. If you are trying to persuade people to save the environment, don't include a paragraph about the school newspaper.)
- Organization and elaboration of details. (There are several details in logical order to support each topic sentence.)
- Logical and cohesive use of transitions. (There are transitions between paragraphs and ideas, and they make sense.)

Sentence Construction

- Syntactic and rhetorical sophistication. (You have used words well and varied the sentence structure.)
- Subordination and coordination. (You have a logical sequence in your sentences and used conjunctions correctly.)
- Avoids wordiness. (You have edited out redundant words and phrases and changed phrases to adjectives where possible.)

Usage

- Knowledge and application of rules, leaving few, if any, errors. (You have used the rules of the English language fairly well; note that a few errors are allowed.)

Mechanics

- Few errors. (Same as above!)

Word Choice

- Consistent use of rich words and images. (Don't go too crazy with this one. Use a specific word instead of a phrase if you can. This is not creative writing, so don't add too many images.)

Although all of that seems overwhelming, it is merely what you do every time you peer edit and revise. You are correcting a piece of writing and making it better.

Additional Information

You will also be given a guide with four editing conventions (things to make it easier to edit). YOU DO NOT HAVE TO USE THESE. If you have learned a different method of editing and are going to rewrite the essay on the lined paper, use this method. If you wish to use the editing marks from the editing guide, then practice using them in your own first drafts so that you do not have to think about them:

The words in the circle are the words you want to move. The arrow shows you where to move these words.

~~Cross out~~
shows that you want to completely get rid of these words.

^ shows that you want to insert a word or several words. You write the words or word above the ^.

Ⓐ tells the reader to go to the section you have labeled *A* and read that text, then to return to this text.

You are doing exactly what you do when you peer edit and revise in your classes, so you have had a lot of practice at this.

HOW TO GO ABOUT REVISING A STUDENT ESSAY

When revising an essay, read through the entire essay first, then work through it paragraph by paragraph.

Step 1: Read the Student Essay

The overall structure should be clear. Each paragraph should support the main idea that the reader is trying to convey.

The first paragraph should be CLEAR.

It should have a statement of the situation so that the reader understands the problem. It should have a statement of the writer's position or idea. Then it should contain the main ideas the writer is going to discuss.

The supporting paragraphs should give specific reasons and examples. The writer should not merely repeat what has already been said in different words.

The concluding paragraph should restate the writer's opinion.

This is a sample editorial that needs to be edited/revised:

School uniforms seem to have numerous advantages for the school district, but few for the students. Teenagers need an avenue to express their individuality and their style of dress is one such avenue. Although schools claim that individual styles often are associated with a particular clique or group, that is also a reflection of the world we live in. If you work in a city you often dress the way other people in the city dress. If you work outside you may not often wear a three piece suit. Adults who must constantly deal with the public dress differently than adults who do not have to deal with the public.

Students are at a stage in their lives where they are attempting to create there own individual identity. The way they choose to dress is one way that they define theirselves. A teen-ager who wears dark clothes may be understood to be part of a certain group, or like specific music; but that is part of who and what they are.

If the school board would stop and think about the effect this would have on the students, they would not try to make us wear uniforms. Students would be angry and that is not a good environment for learning to take place. Students would have to purchase numerous uniforms and they would never wear them anywhere else, so it would be expensive and parents would be angry. There are certainly other ways to deal with cliques and groups in schools than to put us all in the same outfit. Perhaps that would seem to be a solution, but it is merely masking the problem.

Step 2: Breaking Down Logic and Structure

Read the following first paragraph and mark the places where the logic and structure need to be improved.

School uniforms seem to have numerous advantages for the school district, but few for the students. Teenagers need an avenue to express their individuality and their style of dress is one such avenue. Although schools claim that individual styles often are associated with a particular clique or group, that is also a reflection of the world we live in. If you work in a city you often dress the way other people in the city dress. If you work outside you may not often wear a three piece suit. Adults who must constantly deal with the public dress differently than adults who do not have to deal with the public.

The above paragraph has two problems. First, it does not contain a clear statement of the problem; the writer immediately begins with his or her opinion. A background statement should be added.

Add: The Graystone School Board is debating whether to mandate school uniforms for its students.

Second, the paragraph goes into too much detail about the issue of dress being associated with a particular group. This detail would be better in a supporting paragraph. This would be a spot to move text.

Continue reading the essay.

The second paragraph has some grammatical problems:

Students are at a stage in their lives where they are attempting to create there own individual identity. The way they choose to dress is one way that they define theirselves. A teen-ager who wears dark clothes may be understood to be part of a certain group, or like specific music; but that is part of who and what they are.

The editing of this paragraph would require that you change

There   to   their
Theirselves   to   themselves
;   to   a ,

If you wish to revise the last sentence, change "who and what they are" to "their identity."

It would also be helpful to add another specific example. One example is seldom enough to convince a reader.

The third paragraph is a paragraph to revise. The wording is poor. The line about the parents does not go along with the topic sentence and should be completely rewritten. The problem is that a paragraph must be centered on one idea:

If the school board would stop and think about the effect this would have on the students, they would not try to make us wear uniforms. Students would be angry and that is not a good environment for learning to take place. Students would have to purchase numerous uniforms and they would never wear them anywhere else, so it would be expensive and parents would be angry.

The first sentence needs to mention both students and parents. A possible revision would be

The school board must consider the negative effects that mandated uniforms would have on both students and parents.

You could leave the second sentence if you wish, or add a cause/effect sentence and change the wording to be more convincing.

The board has struggled to create a positive learning experience for its students; required uniforms would anger students and create a hostile environment.

The next sentence could be broken into two components:

Uniforms could not be worn anywhere else and so they are not a good clothing invest-ment. Yet, purchasing multiple uniforms would be expensive and parents would be upset.

It would be a good idea to add another sentence to this paragraph, but it is not necessary. To revise the following paragraph:

There are certainly other ways to deal with cliques and groups in schools than to put us all in the same outfit. Perhaps that would seem to be a solution, but it is merely masking the problem.

This would actually be better developed as a body paragraph. It introduces a new idea that is not developed. The final paragraph should restate the opinion, not introduce a new idea.

SENTENCE CONSTRUCTION

In editing, you will probably see more run-on sentences than sentence fragments. Most sentence fragments are obvious and start with a conjunction:

But not enough students wear them.

The above is a sentence fragment because it is not a complete thought. It is more likely that you will see sentences that are too long to be clear:

I understand that the school board believes that they cannot make uniforms optional because then they think that not enough students would want to wear them and the stu-dents would dress the same as they do now.

If you have to take a breath when you read this sentence out loud, then break it into two or more sentences. The major problem with the above sentence is that it uses too many words to express each thought:

Revised: The school board believes that students would not wear uniforms if they were optional. There would be no change in student dress.

There is a review of mechanics and usage conventions in this chapter. Use this review as practice for the revise/edit section of the HSPA.

HOW WILL YOU BE SCORED?

There will be two readers for the revise/edit essay response. Each reader can assign a maximum of 4 points to your essay. The two readers scores will be added together for a maximum of 8 points for this task.

MECHANICS AND USAGE CONVENTIONS

The following section reviews the most frequently made mistakes in student writing. It will help you prepare to tackle the Revise/Edit section of the HSPA.

Mechanics (Homonyms)

These are the words from which spell check can't save you! Homonyms are often used in editing tests and are worth remembering. If you have never used homonyms correctly, this is a good time to learn.

The Frequent Mistakes

They're, their, there	*They're* is the easy one. It is the contraction of *they are*. Example: *They're going to the store.*
	Their refers to people. It has an "I" in it; remember "I" is a person. Example: *Their house is painted yellow.*
	There is a place. It has the word *here* in it. Put the *t* in front of *here* and you get *there*. Example: *The house is over there, next to the red one.*
Its, it's	*Its* is actually possessive. If you want to show ownership, use *its*. Example: *The cat licked its paws.*
	It's is a contraction of *it is*. If you have trouble with these two, just always use *it is* and *its*, and never use the apostrophe. Example: *It's sometimes difficult to study when your friends are going out.*
To, too, two	Many students use *to* correctly. *I am going to the store; I'll be back in an hour.*
	Too causes confusion. It means *in addition to* or *also*. Remember that it has an extra *o* in addition to the original *o*. Example: *He ordered ice cream too.*
	Two is the number (2). Example: *There are two ways to work through that problem.*
Your, You're	*Your* means it belongs to you. Example: *Is that your jacket on the chair?*
	You're is a contraction for *you are*. Example: *You're really good at math!*

Other Homonyms

Affect (verb)	The explosion *affected* her hearing.
Effect (noun)	The *effect* of the explosion was that she could not hear for weeks.
Already	Refers to time. Example: We have *already* done that.
All ready	Example: We are *all ready* to go.
Altar	A spot where religious rituals are performed. Example: The *altar* was at the front of the church.
Alter	To change. Example: *Alter* the directions; there is a detour on that street.
Altogether	Completely or entirely. Example: That statement is *altogether* wrong.

All together	Everyone in the same place. Example: The family is *all together* for the first time in a year.
Brake	To stop or slow down. The mechanism used to stop or slow down. Example: You are going too fast. Step on the *brake*.
Break	To do something that causes an item to no longer function. Example: The little boy should not *break* his brother's CDs.
Capital	The city that is the seat of government. Example: Trenton is the *capital* of New Jersey. Punishable by death. Example: *Capital* punishment is a controversial issue.
Capitol	A building. Example: It is easy to pick out the *capitol* in Trenton.
Coarse	Not fine or smooth. Example: Sand is *coarse* and irritating.
Course	Series of classes about one subject. Example: The psychology *course* was very interesting.
Complement	Something that completes. Example: His ability to revise *complement*s my ability to write first drafts.
Compliment	(Noun): A positive remark about a person or event. Example: She was pleased by his *compliment*. (Verb): The act of saying or writing something good about a person or event. Example: He *complimented* her performance.
Council	A group that has a specific task (people). Example: The township voted in a new *council*.
Counsel	Advice, giving advice. (A person who gives you advice is a counselor.) Example: My guidance *counselor* helped me decide on a college.
Desert	(Noun): A region that has little rain. Have you ever been to the Sahara *desert*? (Verb): To leave. Example: In the time of war, soldiers have been known to *desert* their troup.
Dessert	A hot fudge sundae, apple pie, etc. Example: My favorite *dessert* is chocolate pudding.
Later	Refers to time. Example: I'll see you *later*.
Latter	Refers to placement (last-mentioned item). Example: The first answer was wrong, but the *latter* answer is correct.
Miner	Someone who works in a mine. Example: He had been a coal *miner* for 20 years.
Minor	Someone who is not 18. Example: A *minor* cannot buy lottery tickets in New Jersey.
Passed	(Verb): To go by something. Example: We just *passed* the exit we were supposed to take.

Past
(Noun/adjective/preposition): A time before.
Example: Her *past* actions did not give us reason to trust her.

Peace
Absence of fighting.
Example: We would like some *peace* and quiet.

Piece
A part of a whole.
Example: That *piece* of cake looks delicious.

Personal
Something that affects an individual.
Example: I think that information is *personal*; I don't share it with strangers.

Personnel
People employed in any work or enterprise.
Example: The *personnel* in your company are an extremely loyal group.

Plain
Not fancy; having little decoration.
Example: The dress is very *plain*; it is all black.
A large stretch of flat land.
Example: Distance is difficult to judge when you are on the *plains* in the Midwest.

Plane
A form of air transportation.
Example: The *plane* to Denver was filled with people.

Principal
A primary person in an organization.
You can remember the rule this way: the person who runs the school is your PAL.
Example: The *principal* made several important announcements before the assembly began.

Principle
An idea in which one firmly believes.
Example: The *principle* on which our country stands is freedom for all.

Stationary
Not moving, in a fixed position.
Example: The unidentified flying object appeared to be *stationary*, as it hovered over the tower.

Stationery
Paper on which letters are written.
Example: I don't like the *stationery* with large flowered borders; there is no room to write.

Than
A word used with comparisons.
Example: Steve is taller *than* Bill even though Bill is older.

Then
A word that refers to time.
Example: We finished our homework, *then* went to the store.

Waist
The middle part of the body.
Example: The exercise program is supposed to take inches off the *waist*.

Waste	(Verb): To squander.
	Example: You just *wasted* an hour online.
	(Noun): Items thrown away.
	Example: The *waste* from that project is ridiculous.
Weather	Rain, snow, sleet, etc.
	Example: The *weather* is supposed to be miserable; take a coat when leaving the house.
Whether	A word used in a manner similar to *if*.
	Example: I don't know *whether* to go out or stay home and try to finish this work.
Who's	The contraction for *who is* or *who has*.
	Example: *Who's* going to the dance?
Whose	This word shows ownership.
	Example: *Whose* book is on the floor?

Subject/Verb Agreement (Usage)

Subject/verb agreement means that if the subject (the main noun) of the sentence is singular (one), then the predicate (main verb) is also singular. If the subject of the sentence is plural, the predicate must be plural.

In most sentences it will be obvious if there is a subject/verb agreement error: it will sound wrong. The sentence would read this way:

Our writing center, according to its teachers, are designed to provide individual writing instruction.

The sentence "sounds wrong" because the subject (writing center) is singular; there is only one. The predicate *are designed* is plural; the word *are* signals that there is more than one.

If a sentence "sounds wrong" and the mistake is not immediately obvious, begin by underlining the subject and predicate and check that they are either both singular or both plural. In most cases you will change the VERB to agree with the subject.

In our example we would change are designed to is designed so that the sentence would become

Our writing center, according to its teachers, is designed to provide individual writing instruction.

> **HINT: Most subject/verb agreement errors occur in sentences with two or more commas.**

Try one of these yourself:

The tiny chips that operate a computer is the source of many computer problems.

1. Underline the subject of the sentence.
2. Underline the predicate of the sentence.
3. Is the subject singular or plural? _____
4. Is the predicate singular or plural? _____

Subject:	CHIPS	*(Plural)*
Predicate:	IS	*(Singular)*

The meaning of the sentence would be altered if the subject were changed, so change the predicate to agree with the subject.

The new sentence reads

The tiny chips that operate a computer are the source of many computer problems.

The Subjects That Become Difficult

The only subjects that are particularly difficult are called indefinite pronouns. Memorize these lists of singular and plural subjects:

Singular

anybody	Is anybody going to the store?
anyone	Has anyone seen Mark today?
each	Each of the horses is fed separately.
either	Either one of the books is a good reference.
everyone	Everyone in the room is upset by his remarks.
everybody	Everybody wishes to go to Boston rather than New York.
neither	Neither Jack nor Mike likes to drive long distances.
no one	No one has volunteered to do that.
somebody	Somebody shut off the air conditioner and it is rather hot.
someone	Someone has to write this report; the chairman of the committee has just been called to Washington.

Plural

both	Both Jack and Mike dislike driving long distances.
few	A few of the people in the room were upset by his remarks.
many	Many of the people in the room were upset by his remarks.
several	Several of the people in the room were upset by his remarks.

Some words can be considered either singular or plural, depending on the sentence:

all	All of the neighbors are concerned about her. (plural)
	All of the neighborhood is concerned about her. (singular)
any	Are any of the grammar books in Room 12? (plural)
	Any book with a grammar section will do. (singular)
most	Most of the students dislike grammar books anyway. (plural)
some	Some of the students find grammar somewhat interesting. (plural)
	Some water is spilling on the floor by the fountain. (singular)

Whether these words are singular or plural depends on the sentence and its meaning. For your purposes, it depends on the noun to which the word is "linked." For example:

Most of the students are going to the dance.

Most is linked to the word *students*. The word *students* is plural. The verb needs to be plural.

> *Example: Most of the article is boring.*

Most is linked to the word *article*. The word *article* is singular. The verb needs to be singular.

TRY IT

Let's try some simple subject/verb agreement editing:

1. Neither Sandra nor Danny were going to the party.
2. The group of thirty musicians were leaving to play in a parade.
3. Some of these mistakes are deliberate.
4. No one in the test audiences like the ending of the film.
5. Editing papers with varying topics are always difficult.

Number one does not, necessarily, sound wrong. However, we know that *neither/nor* is singular so *were* needs to be changed to *was*.

Number two is incorrect. The subject is *group*, which is singular. The verb needs to be singular. (The group of thirty musicians was leaving to play in a parade.)

Number three should sound correct and it is. *Some* is linked to *mistakes*. *Mistakes* is a plural form; therefore the verb needs to be plural.

Number four should "sound" wrong. The problem with a sentence like number four is that it is often read correctly even when the words on the paper are incorrect; the reader automatically changes it. Be careful to read what is actually written. ("No one in the test audiences"—*no one* is singular. *Like* is plural. Change the verb to agree with the noun.)

The sentence should read *No one in the test audiences likes the ending of the film.*

Your language "ear" should tell you that number five is wrong. (Editing papers with varying topics is always difficult.) If you are having problems determining what is wrong, delete all the words between the subject and the predicate. You would then have *Editing are always difficult.* It is easier to see that you have a singular subject and a plural verb.

Pronoun Antecedent Agreement (Usage)

The next popular error is a pronoun antecedent error. Practice in editing for this error is a good idea because it will make these mistakes easy to spot.

Pronouns take the place of a noun.

Nominative Case	Objective Case	Possessive Case
I	me	my, mine
you	you	your, yours
he, she, it	him, her, it	his, her, hers, its
we	us	our, ours
you	you	you, your
they	them	their, theirs

Because these words take the place of a noun, they have to be the same gender and number as the noun they replace. That means that if an author is writing about Jerry, a sixteen-year-old boy, that writer cannot use *she* in the next sentence to refer to Jerry. *She* refers to a female, so the pronoun is not the same gender as the noun it is replacing. A writer cannot use *they* because Jerry is one person and *they* is plural; the pronoun would not agree in number with the noun.

Do not change the noun in a pronoun antecedent error; change the pronoun. So in the incorrect sentence

During warm weather, warm-blooded animals must find itself shade in order to keep cool

change the pronoun *itself* to agree in number with *animals*. (Change *itself* to *themselves*.)

If you find that you have trouble finding pronoun antecedent errors, highlight all the pronouns. Then look at whether they agree with the nouns they are replacing.

Indefinite or Ambiguous Pronouns (Usage)

This means that it is impossible to tell which noun the pronoun is replacing. For example:

Mrs. Smith brought her daughter to camp at 9:30. John reported that he told her that he would take Jane to her group and she said she would instead.

There are too many pronouns in this sentence. It is not clear which person is the antecedent. Rather than struggle to fix a hopeless sentence, rewrite it.

Mrs. Smith brought her daughter to camp at 9:30. John reported that he offered to bring Jane to her group; however, Mrs. Smith said she would bring Jane.

Your turn!
Revise the following sentence:

Those who had land and crops lured the hungry with money to make their own big profits.

_____

_____

_____

Parallel Structure (Sentence Construction/Usage)

Parallel structure errors generally occur when there are words in a series:

Example: Running, kicking, walking

These words are parallel. They are the same form of each word.

Example: They taught skating, nutrition and to physical condition at the center.

This sentence is not parallel. *Skating* is a noun that names a subject that the center teaches. *Nutrition* is a noun that names a subject that the center teaches. *To physical condition* is NOT a noun that names a subject taught. Therefore, the sentence is not parallel.

Rewrite: They taught skating, nutrition, and physical education at the center.

HINT: Whenever you have two or more commas in the same line, look for parallel construction.

Be certain that verbs are all the same tense. Do not mix tenses in a series.

You try it!

The students stole the test, duplicated it, and

_____

_____

The next verb must be past tense since the other two are past tense.

Faulty Comparison (Usage)

Many of the comparisons that are made as we speak are grammatically incorrect. That makes it difficult to edit a written piece because it sounds right to our language ear. Whenever you see a word that ends in *er* or *est*, check to see that it is the correct form of comparison.

Comparisons (similarities or differences between two things, or similarities or differences among more than two things) are generally formed by adding either *er* or *est* to the end of the word, or adding *more/less*, *most/least* in front of the word. NEVER add a word at the front and an ending at the back.

er	Use *er* when you are comparing two things.
est	Use *est* when you are comparing more than two things.
more/less	Use *more/less* when you are comparing two things.
most/least	Use *most/least* when you are comparing more than two things.

He is the most handsome young man in the room.
She is the prettiest girl in the room.

(You are comparing the boy or girl with many others.)

He is the more handsome of the two brothers.
She is prettier than her sister.

(You are comparing the boy or girl with one other person.)

Idiomatic Expressions

An idiomatic expression is simply a group of words that go together and have a generally accepted meaning. Idiomatic expressions are not based upon rules or logic; they just ARE. Many idiomatic expressions are dependent on the last word of the expression to determine their meaning. The expressions using *turn* are a good example:

Some idiomatic expressions using the word *turn*:

turn away	One meaning is to literally turn around and face the other direction. The second meaning is to refuse to allow someone to enter a place.
	Example: The students were turned away because the dance was canceled.
turn back	To physically reverse direction.
	Example: There had been a mudslide in the Rockies and the road was closed.
	We had to turn back.
no turning back	Generally means to continue a course of action.
	Example: Once we had decided on the theme for the yearbook, there was no turning back.
turn down	To refuse.
	Example: The principal turned down the student council request for an open campus policy.
turn into	To physically move in a certain direction.
	Example: When we got lost, we had to turn into a gas station and ask for directions.
	To change.
	Example: The princess kissed the frog and he turned into a prince.
turn over	To change position.
	Example: The sled turned over when we were halfway down the hill.
turn up	To appear.
	Example: Don't worry, your car keys will turn up somewhere.

Because you have an opportunity to rewrite the student piece for clarity, you can simply change expressions that do not make sense. Be sure to understand the meaning of the sentence first.

Possessives (Spelling)

This means that the reader is able to understand that the first noun owns, or possesses, the second noun. So in *Barbara's car* Barbara owns the car.

The trick is to remember that an *s* should be placed on the end of the word; if the *s* is already there, don't add one. If the *s* is not already there, add one.

Singular Nouns:

Add an '*s*	Barbara (one person = singular)
	+
	the car that belongs to Barbara
	=
	Barbara's car

Technically, if the noun is more than one syllable and ends in an *s* sound (*princess*) there is a choice. Add *'s* or just put an *'* after the *s*.

princess' castle   or   princess's castle

Either one should be considered correct. However, most of us prefer *princess'*, and many people are taught that it is the only correct way to form this possessive—it is easier just to add the *'*.

Plural nouns:

If a plural noun ends in *s* (and most do), just add an apostrophe (*'*).

dogs' toys	dogs (there are several dogs = plural)
	+
	the toys that belong (*'*) to the dogs
	=
	dogs' toys

If a plural noun does not end in an *s*, add *'s*.

children's toys	children (there are several little people = plural)
	+
	the toys that belong ('s) to the children
	=
	children's toys

Punctuation (Mechanics)

The majority of punctuation is not too complicated.

We all use a question mark at the end of a question.   ?

We all use periods at the end of a sentence.   .

Most of us use commas to separate items in a series.   ,

Using a colon or a semicolon can be confusing.
Let's look at the colon (:) first, since it is the easier one.

Colon (:)

- You use a colon before a list.
- You need to be aware of several potential mistakes: subject/verb agreement, pronoun antecedent errors, parallel structure errors, and faulty comparison errors.

(Naturally, there is an exception to this rule. If the list follows a verb or a preposition, you do not use a colon.)

Example: The United Nations sent food, clothing, and medicine to the war zone. (The list follows the verb sent, so do not use a colon.)

Example: Steve was fascinated with wolves, mountain lions, and other predators. (The list follows the preposition with, so do not use a colon.)

Semicolon (;)

Use a semicolon when joining two independent clauses. This means that each part of the sentence (before and after the semicolon) can stand alone as a sentence.

Example: The shore was extremely crowded; people wanted to sunbathe rather than swim.

Each part of this sentence could be a sentence by itself. Whether to use two sentences or to join them with a semicolon is a writing decision and depends upon the effect the writer wants and the other sentence structures the writer has used.

DO NOT use a semicolon when the second part of the sentence begins with

and	nor
but	for
or	yet

The majority of the time the use of these words makes the second part of the sentence an incomplete thought.

Example: The shore was extremely crowded, but there were few people in the water.

TRY SOME REVISING/EDITING

1 In both *The Grapes of Wrath*, by John Steinbeck, and *The Natural*, by Bernard Malamud, there were incidents of tragic heroes that take place.

Can there be "incidents" of tragic heroes? What word could you use instead? What words are redundant and can be removed?

Rewrite the sentence:

_____

_____

_____

(There are tragic heroes in both Steinbeck's *The Grapes of Wrath* and Malamud's *The Natural*.)

2 Society does not allow them to be successful due to the greediness and selfishness that society has.

Try changing the prepositional phrase. The sentence needs to be revised completely, not edited.

_____

_____

_____

(They cannot be successful because of society's selfishness and greed.)

3 The societies in which the two works are based on are the materialistic people who surround the main characters.

There are numerous problems here. First, determine the idea of the sentence.

> *Idea:* *Two works*
> *Societies = materialistic people*
> *Materialistic people surround the main characters.*

Take the long, wordy phrase and change it to an adjective when revising this sentence.

_____

_____

_____

(In both works, the main characters live in materialistic societies.)

Try to revise/edit these sentences:

1 In *The Grapes of Wrath*, the bank forecloses on the Joad's house and the owners wanted to shut down government camps which helped people.

(Hint: Look at the verbs.)

_____

_____

_____

2 The bank doesn't care that the Joads will have no home, it just cares about it's profit.

(Hint: Are there two independent clauses? Are the homonyms correct?)

_____

_____

_____

3 This is thought by the farmers when the bank representatives came to the farms.

(Hint: Bracket the prepositional phrases. Now put the sentence in conventional order.)

_____

_____

_____

4 Both books illustrate the selfishness of various forces as it works against the goodness of the main characters.

(Hint: Edit for pronoun agreement. You might want to find a better word for *goodness*.)

_____

_____

5 She grew up in a culture, which did not value the life of a female, as much as that of a male.

(Hint: punctuation)

_____

_____

_____

6 Finally, Dimmesdale and Chillingworth had a similar balanced relationship.

(Hint: What type of word modifies an adjective?)

_____

_____

_____

7 Our towns security system always makes people feel comfortable.

(Hint: What belongs to what?)

_____

_____

_____

8 It must be reminded also that any new position requires extensive additional training.

(Hint: What word is used incorrectly? Where would you add punctuation?)

_____

_____

_____

9 Its fast, convenient, and saves time.

(Hint: Check parallel structure. Check homonyms.)

_____

_____

_____

Practice revising and editing your own writing!

PUTTING IT ALL TOGETHER: SAMPLE REVISING AND EDITING TASK

Your town has become increasingly concerned about the number of teenagers who are out late at night. The town council is debating the issue of imposing a curfew. The curfew would require that anyone under the age of eighteen could not be out after 11 P.M. There are many citizens who support the curfew and many who do not.

A seventeen-year-old student has written an editorial for the local paper expressing his views on the proposed curfew. Read the first draft and decide how to improve the meaning and clarity of the text. Then make your revisions.

My opinion about this curfew is that it is unfair to the older teen-agers. There are many responsible teen-agers who have good reason to be out after this time of night. Some of us have jobs and work until just before the curfews. And there are alot of school activityes which don't end until after the curfew.

With the current economy, many teenagers have to work after school. Jobs often end before the curfew but we still have to get home. Those of us whom work in town and walk home won't be able to get there before 11 o clock. That would leave us with a major problems: do we quit our job or do we go against the curfew?

This problem would also refer to school activities. Dances usually end at about 11 o'clock because that gives the students enough time to get to the dance and be there for awhile before the end. Even basketball games sometimes end after this curfew. Would the coaches stop a basketball game because it is necessary to send everybody home since there is a curfew in our town? How would the other teams feel about this?

My conclusion is that this requirement cannot be accepted by the town because it would really have a bad effect on the teen-agers and on other teen-agers as well.

(This is a piece to rewrite. Remember that you are not changing the opinion of the writer. You are clarifying the writer's opinion.)

In the test you will be given two pieces of lined paper in the answer booklet that you may use to rewrite the piece. For this exercise we want you to rewrite the editorial on the following pages.

REVISION

_____

_____

_____

_____

_____

_____

_____

_____

_____

_____

Chapter 7

Sample Practice Tests in Language Arts Literacy

Here are two full-length HSPA-type practice tests in Language Arts Literacy. Each test has the five components of the HSPA test. After you have completed the practice sections found earlier in this book, practice with a full-length test.

Find a quiet place to take this test. It should be a place without distractions. Be sure to time yourself according to the specified length for each portion of the test. Between each part of the test get up and stretch for about five minutes. In the real HSPA, you will have two days to complete the Language Arts Literacy sections. You may want to do the same thing when you practice at home.

When you have completed all sections of the test, check your answers against the answer key provided. If there was a portion of the test with which you had difficulty, go back to that section in this book and review the material again.

Good luck! If you have practiced all the samples in this book, you should succeed quite nicely on the "real" HSPA.

PRACTICE TEST 1
Answer Sheets

PART 1—PICTURE PROMPT WRITING TASK

Remember: This page will not be scored.

PREWRITING/PLANNING SPACE

ANSWER SHEET FOR PICTURE PROMPT WRITING TASK

ANSWER SHEET FOR PICTURE PROMPT WRITING TASK (continued)

PART 2—NARRATIVE READING

MULTIPLE-CHOICE QUESTIONS

1. Ⓐ Ⓑ Ⓒ Ⓓ
2. Ⓐ Ⓑ Ⓒ Ⓓ
3. Ⓐ Ⓑ Ⓒ Ⓓ
4. Ⓐ Ⓑ Ⓒ Ⓓ

5. Ⓐ Ⓑ Ⓒ Ⓓ
6. Ⓐ Ⓑ Ⓒ Ⓓ
7. Ⓐ Ⓑ Ⓒ Ⓓ

8. Ⓐ Ⓑ Ⓒ Ⓓ
9. Ⓐ Ⓑ Ⓒ Ⓓ
10. Ⓐ Ⓑ Ⓒ Ⓓ

11. NARRATIVE READING OPEN-ENDED RESPONSE

_____

_____

_____

_____

_____

_____

_____

_____

_____

_____

_____

_____

_____

_____

_____

_____

_____

_____

_____

11. NARRATIVE READING OPEN-ENDED RESPONSE (continued)

_____

_____

_____

_____

_____

_____

_____

_____

_____

_____

_____

_____

_____

_____

_____

_____

_____

_____

_____

_____

_____

_____

_____

_____

12. NARRATIVE READING OPEN-ENDED RESPONSE

12. NARRATIVE READING OPEN-ENDED RESPONSE (continued)

PART 3—PERSUASIVE WRITING TASK

PREWRITING/PLANNING SPACE

Remember: This page will not be scored.

ANSWER SHEET FOR PERSUASIVE WRITING TASK

ANSWER SHEET FOR PERSUASIVE WRITING TASK (continued)

ANSWER SHEET FOR PERSUASIVE WRITING TASK (continued)

ANSWER SHEET FOR PERSUASIVE WRITING TASK (continued)

PART 4—PERSUASIVE READING

MULTIPLE-CHOICE QUESTIONS

1. Ⓐ Ⓑ Ⓒ Ⓓ   5. Ⓐ Ⓑ Ⓒ Ⓓ   8. Ⓐ Ⓑ Ⓒ Ⓓ
2. Ⓐ Ⓑ Ⓒ Ⓓ   6. Ⓐ Ⓑ Ⓒ Ⓓ   9. Ⓐ Ⓑ Ⓒ Ⓓ
3. Ⓐ Ⓑ Ⓒ Ⓓ   7. Ⓐ Ⓑ Ⓒ Ⓓ   10. Ⓐ Ⓑ Ⓒ Ⓓ
4. Ⓐ Ⓑ Ⓒ Ⓓ

11. PERSUASIVE READING OPEN-ENDED RESPONSE

_____

_____

_____

_____

_____

_____

_____

_____

_____

_____

_____

_____

_____

_____

_____

_____

_____

_____

_____

_____

_____

11. PERSUASIVE READING OPEN-ENDED RESPONSE (continued)

12. PERSUASIVE READING OPEN-ENDED RESPONSE

12. PERSUASIVE READING OPEN-ENDED RESPONSE (continued)

PART 5—REVISE/EDIT STUDENT TEXT

REVISE/EDIT STUDENT TEXT (continued)

WRITER'S CHECKLIST

Content/Organization

☐ 1. Your focus should be on the purpose of your writing and the audience for whom you are writing.

☐ 2. You should support your point of view with specific details and evidence.

☐ 3. The order and structure of your ideas will help communicate your view.

Sentence Construction

☐ 1. Use varied sentence structure.

☐ 2. Check that you do not have sentence fragments.

☐ 3. Check that you do not have run-on sentences.

Usage

☐ 1. Choose your words carefully so that you convey the meaning clearly.

☐ 2. Check that words have been used in the correct context.

Mechanics

☐ 1. Capitalize, spell, and punctuate correctly.

REVISING-EDITING GUIDE

You will also be given a guide with four editing conventions (things to make it easier to edit). YOU DO NOT HAVE TO USE THESE. If you have learned a different method of editing and are going to rewrite the essay on the lined paper, use this method. If you wish to use the editing marks from the editing guide, then practice using them in your own first drafts so that you do not have to think about them:

1.

   The words in the circle are the words you want to move. The arrow shows you where to move these words.

2. ~~Cross out~~

   shows that you want to completely get rid of these words.

3. ^ shows that you want to insert a word or several words. You write the words or word above the ^.

4. Ⓐ tells the reader to go to the section you have labeled *A* and read that text, then to return to this text.

You are doing exactly what you do when you peer edit and revise in your classes, so you have had a lot of practice at this.

PRACTICE TEST 1

NJ HSPA LANGUAGE ARTS LITERACY—DAY 1
PART 1

Directions: Today you are going to take part of the High School Proficiency Assessment for Language Arts Literacy. The assessment contains different types of text and different activities. In the first part of the test, you will look at a picture and then complete a writing task. In this activity, you have an opportunity to demonstrate how well you can organize and express your ideas in written text. Refer to the Writer's Checklist of important points to remember as you write. Educators who read your writing will consider these important points when they read and score your writing.

You will have 30 minutes to complete the writing task. Take a few minutes to think about the task and to plan what you want to say before you begin to write. You may use the prewriting/planning space to plan your text, but your prewriting will not be scored. **Only your writing on the lined pages of your answer sheet will be scored.** Do your best to make your writing clear and well organized. Keep your purpose in mind as you write and use your checklist.

You must use a No. 2 pencil. You may either print or write your final copy. You may *not* use a dictionary or any other reference materials during the test. However, you may use the Writer's Checklist. If you finish before the time is called, review what you have written using the Writer's Checklist to read critically and improve what you have written.

An ancient proverb says, "A picture is worth a thousand words." Regardless of the artist's original intent, what we see in the picture can be very different from what others see. What story does this picture tell you? Use your imagination and experience to speculate about what is happening. Then write your story.

NJ HSPA LANGUAGE ARTS LITERACY—DAY 1
PART 2

Directions: In this part of the test, you will read a narrative passage and then respond to the multiple-choice and open-ended questions that follow it. You may look back at the passage and make notes in the margin if you like, but you must record your answers on your answer sheet.

You will have 50 minutes for this part of the test.

The following is an excerpt from *Here at Eagle Pond*. So often, memories that lie dormant in our minds affect us in significant ways. Donald Hall's memoir reminds us of the interconnections among all things on this earth.

PERENNIALS
by Donald Hall

1   I live in the house I always wanted to live in. When I was a boy, spending summers here with my grandmother and grandfather, I wrote poems and read books in the morning; in the afternoon I played with my grandfather, listening to his long, slow stories of old times. I loved him, and he gave me the past of his boyhood as if it were a fortune or a mild chronic disease. Over the years of separation, in a suburban world, I felt continuously connected with this land and with the dead who make it precious. Now I return full circle, except that I write all day and I do not hay at all. If I miss my grandfather and his stories, I do not miss him so much as I used to; he died long ago but he is no longer *missing*. As I reach the age he carried when I was born, I sleep in the bed he died in and I find him everywhere I look. In a cousin's cheekbone, in a turn of phrase, in a remembered quilt I find him.

2   Paul Fenton reminds me of my grandfather, with good reason. Paul's mother was Wesley's sister Grace, who died just three years ago. Paul is seventy now, a pacemaker in his chest, and he complains that although he can still chop wood all day, now he must pause

sometimes to catch his breath, and the doctor can't tell him why. When I was a boy on the farm, my grandfather was in his sixties and seventies, while Paul was early in middle age. Paul and Bertha used to call on Wesley and Kate; my grandfather saved good stories for Paul, who liked hearing his uncle's talk. Now sometimes Bertha and Paul will call on us, driving over from the long farm where their son Dennis keeps fifty Holsteins, and Paul has a story to tell me.

3   When Paul was a boy, an old man told him this one, and the old man told Paul that he had heard it from an old man when *he* was a boy.

4   "So this one goes back some . . .

5   "Once there was a man living around here who filled his ox cart every year in the fall.* He filled it with everything he and his family made over the whole year: things his wife and daughters sewed or knitted or crocheted, things like yarn and cloth, goose feathers for stuffing beds, linen and flax seed. Probably the man and his boys made shingles he put in the ox cart; young boys made birch brooms. And he put in the ox cart everything from his fields that would keep and that he didn't need: extra

Go On ➡

apples, potatoes, Indian corn, turnips, pumpkins, and squash; vinegar, honey in combs, dried meat, and maybe tanned deerhide.

6   "Well, he filled it right up with everything all of them had made or done or grown, leaving behind just enough for them to eat and wear all winter. Then he walked beside his ox, ten days maybe, all the way to Portsmouth, where there was a big market. (One year he went all the way down to Boston, to the market by the harbor.) When he got to market he sold whatever he had. There'd be sailors in Portsmouth then, and people came from all around to do their shopping. After he sold his potatoes he sold the bag he brought the potatoes in. If he had vinegar in a barrel, you know he'd've made the barrel too; so then he sold the barrel.

7   "When he sold everything out of his cart, and the cart was empty, he sold the cart. After he sold the cart he sold his ox, harness and all." Paul pauses a moment, grinning, and looks at me to see how I like his story's twist. I like it. Paul goes on.

8   "Then he walked home. Maybe he bought things for his family with the money. Salt, an orange for each of them—they never saw oranges in those days—maybe needles or knives, things he couldn't make at his own forge. But he had his year's money, money for the year.

9   "Then when he came home he started everything over again, the young ox in the barn, the harness, the cart . . ."

10   Paul smiles, excitement in his face; he knows what he has given. Soon he must stand and leave, back to the chores by which he helps Dennis, his necktie and white shirt back in the closet until Sunday. He will wear overalls again, become farmer again—winter and summer, garden and cattlebarn.

11   He leaves me to early November nightfall and my dream of the ox-cart man. I see him walking home from Portsmouth Market, up Highway 4 from Concord through Penacook, Boscawen, Salisbury, Andover. On a narrow dirt road he walks steadily, coins heavy in his pockets, past forest and farm, pasture and cornfield, big houses and settlers' cabins. Now he walks through West Andover, almost home, and I see him down the road in the cool afternoon sun, slanting low from Vermont, lengthening shadows of cornstalks blackened with frost. Now he is home—it is this farm, as I dream it—and his family gathers around him as he gives each of them a gift from his great pockets, needles and combs for the women, a Barlow knife for each boy, and stashes the cash in the treasury crock, which he keeps under a stone in the rootcellar. Now they sit in the dark parlor in December, the family on chairs in a semicircle around the castiron stove, under high candles, working. The ox-cart man sews a harness. His wife and girl children sew, knit, spin, weave. His boys work with leather, carve, whittle. They work, and the years move on in paths and circles of work. From the dark underground of dead winter the year moves to wood-chopping, ice cutting, deer hunting, tanning, coopering, sugaring, manuring, plowing, planting, weeding, haying, harvesting, slaughtering, and filling the cart again, for the journey to Portsmouth.

12   I see that the ox-cart man is a perennial plant, divesting himself each year of everything grown, and growing it all again. When I dream his face I see Paul's face, who harvests a story for me, and I see my grandfather's face, who divested himself of everything he could gather, in his stewardship carrying all the past through winter darkness into present light. I understand: This duty is my duty also. If people like Wesley and Kate, like Paul and Bertha, not only live out their lives but pass on the stories of their lives—their own and the stories dead people told them—by these stories our seasons on earth may return and repeat themselves in others.

13   Let the curve of my story meet the curve of your own.

* After I heard Paul's story, I spent two years making a poem called "Ox-Cart Man," which I printed in *Kicking the Leaves*; I changed one word for *Old and New Poems*. When I had finished the poem I told the same story, in different words, to make the children's book *Ox-Cart Man*, which Barbara Cooney illustrated and which won her the Caldecott Medal in 1981. In "Keeping Things" I told about building a new bathroom. It was expensive, and over its door I've set a plaque: *Caldecott Room*.

Directions for multiple-choice questions 1 through 10:	Read the passage and record your answers on the answer sheet provided.

1 The first paragraph is significant to the story because
   A it reveals that the narrator's grandfather has died.
   B it introduces the central theme of the story.
   C it reveals that there will be a first-person narrator.
   D it reveals that the narrator's cousin resembles the grandfather.

2 The tone of this story can best be described as
   A melancholy
   B informative
   C cynical
   D reminiscent

3 In paragraph 1, the narrator says that now "I do not hay at all." In this context he means that
   A he is not a landowner like his grandfather.
   B he is not a farmer like his grandfather.
   C he does not look like his grandfather.
   D he misses his boyhood summers.

4 The narrator says of his grandfather, ". . . he gave me the past of his boyhood as if it were a fortune or a mild chronic disease." By this he is inferring that
   A his grandfather was often sick as a young child.
   B his grandfather was extremely rich.
   C his grandfather was senile and remembered only his boyhood.
   D his grandfather loved to talk of his past, and his stories became the narrator's inheritance.

5 Why do you think Paul tells the narrator the story of the ox-cart man?
   A Paul thinks of giving stories as a gift to the narrator.
   B Paul needs an excuse to take Bertha for a drive on Sunday.
   C Paul wants to remind the narrator of the days with his grandfather.
   D Paul doesn't want the narrator to forget the ox-cart man.

6 In paragraph 11, what is the effect of listing all the things that the ox-cart man and his family do throughout the year?
   A It emphasizes how hard the ox-cart man works.
   B It emphasizes the line "the years move on in paths and circles of work."
   C It emphasizes the narrator's imagination after Paul leaves.
   D It emphasizes the line "When he got to market he sold whatever he had."

7 In paragraph 12, the narrator says that the ox-cart man is a "perennial plant." This is an example of which literary device?
   A A simile
   B A metaphor
   C An oxymoron
   D Exaggeration

Go On ➡

8 The narrator says that Paul has "harvested" a story for him. The narrator means that
  A Paul invented this tale just for him.
  B Paul recalled the story from his past and presented it in his own way as a gift to the narrator.
  C Paul told this story because it was about a farmer.
  D this was the final story Paul knew to tell.

9 In paragraph 12, when the narrator says, "This duty is my duty also," he means that
  A his job is to be a farmer like his grandfather and his uncle.
  B his duty is to connect with the land like the ox-cart man.
  C his duty is to remember Wesley, Kate, Paul, and Bertha when they die.
  D his duty is to remember and pass along the past through stories and memories.

10 Which BEST describes what the narrator means when he says, "Let the curve of my story meet the curve of your own"?
  A His story has come full circle.
  B His story is circular like the earth.
  C The reader should connect, through experience and knowledge, with the central theme of his story.
  D The reader should repeat this story to everyone he or she meets to keep the circle going.

Directions for open-ended questions 11 and 12:	Write your response in the space provided on the answer sheet.

11 This short story is really a story within a story.
  • Identify two ways the author has connected the ox-cart man's story with the life of the narrator.
  • How can the ox-cart man and the narrator's grandfather be compared to "Perennials"?

12 According to the narrator, we all have a duty to pass on stories we have heard and stories we have lived.
  • What has the narrator done to pass along the story of the ox-cart man?
  • What story/lesson from your own life do you think it might be your duty to pass along to future generations?

NJ HSPA LANGUAGE ARTS LITERACY—DAY 2
PART 3

Directions: In this part of the test, you will complete a persuasive writing task. You will have an opportunity to demonstrate how well you can organize and express your ideas in written text. Refer to the Writer's Checklist of important points to remember as you write. Educators who read your writing will consider these important points when they read and score your writing.

You will have 60 minutes to complete this writing task. Take a few minutes to think about the task and to plan what you want to say before you begin to write. You may use the prewriting/planning space to plan your text, but your prewriting will not be scored. Do your best to make your writing clear and well organized. Keep your audience and purpose in mind as you write and use your checklist.

You must use a No. 2 pencil. You may either print or write your final copy. You may *not* use a dictionary or any other reference materials during the test. However, you may use the Writer's Checklist. If you finish before the time is called, review what you have written using the Writer's Checklist to read critically and improve what you have written.

WRITING SITUATION

Recent reports have called attention to the high risk of bringing students on class trips. After reexamining its policy, the local school board has proposed eliminating school-sponsored trips off school grounds. This issue has become quite controversial among students, parents, teachers, and the entire community.

In response to all the publicity, the school board has agreed to postpone a decision for two weeks. Meanwhile, the board has invited any concerned individuals to write to them to express views on this subject.

WRITING TASK

Write a letter to the school board either supporting or opposing the proposal to eliminate school-sponsored field trips. Support your position with reasons, examples, facts, and/or other evidence.

NJ HSPA LANGUAGE ARTS LITERACY—DAY 2
PART 4

Practice Test 1

> **Directions:** In this part of the test, you will read a narrative passage and then respond to the multiple-choice and open-ended questions that follow it. You may look back at the passage and make notes in the margin if you like, but you must record your answers on your answer sheet.
>
> You will have 45 minutes for this part of the test.

There are many ways to acquire a household pet, even if you do not have money to purchase one! This article explains the benefits of pet adoption and may give you something to consider if you are in the market to buy a pet.

Adopting a Companion Animal

1   Adopting a cat or dog is not a decision that should be taken lightly. Anyone considering adopting a companion animal should seriously consider the lifelong commitment involved. Don't forget that dogs may live 12 to 15 years and cats even longer—15 to 18 years or more.

2   Do some research about various breeds and species, so you know which ones are best suited to your lifestyle. Evaluate your budget before adopting. Veterinary care (even for a healthy animal: yearly wellness exams, vaccinations, and flea and heartworm control products), obedience classes, pet food, grooming supplies, bedding, litter, and toys add up to a lot more than you might think.

3   Once you have made a well-informed decision to adopt a companion animal, visit your local animal control shelter or humane society first. Even if you are looking for a specific breed, you may be able to find it at your local shelter. You can also adopt from a breed rescue group. Rescue groups exist for virtually every breed of dog and cat. Your humane society or animal control agency can provide you with a list of rescue groups in your area, and many groups also have web sites on the Internet—or call API for more information.

4   Remember that puppies and kittens find homes more easily than older animals, so please consider adopting an adolescent or adult. Mature animals are often house- or litter-box trained, and they may have had some training, or at least have learned some manners. You can avoid the destructive behavior associated with teething. And, you can tell what type of disposition the animal has, since his personality is already fully developed.

5   Many shelters and humane societies now require surgical sterilization prior to adoption. This strict policy is gradually helping to reduce pet overpopulation, and in the last few years we are finally seeing a decline in the number of healthy, adoptable animals being euthanized. If your new companion is not already sterilized, do make arrangements for the surgery as soon as possible.

6   Please do not purchase your companion animal from a pet store, backyard breeder, Internet site, auction, or newspaper ad. Instead, save a life by adopting from a local shelter or breed rescue group. Contrary to what you may have heard, even older dogs can learn at least one new trick—being your loving and loyal companion.

The Problems with Purebreds

7   Purebreds are man-made, "designer" dogs and cats. Mating animals with similar genetics and bloodlines increases the chance that their offspring will inherit the specific traits that are standard for that breed's appearance. However, to produce the diverse looks of cats and dogs that we see today, the health and well-being of the animals themselves have been largely ignored.

8   Purebred animals often suffer from geneti-cally-based health problems, which range from annoying to life-threatening. Basset Hounds, Dachshunds, and other short-legged dogs with long bodies often have back problems. Many Maine Coon cats die at a young age from severe heart disease. The female Bulldog's pelvis is too small to give birth normally—all puppies must be delivered by cesarian section. Persian cats often have difficulty breathing and chronic eye discharges. Giant breed dogs, like Great Pyre-nees, Irish Wolfhounds, and Great Danes, are prone to bone cancer as well as heart disease. Hip dysplasia—and the pain and disability that go along with it—has a significant genetic com-ponent.

9   Temperament and behavior problems may also result from breeding for a certain look without regard to other traits that may accom-pany those looks. For instance, Labrador and Golden Retrievers used to be known for their calm, placid dispositions, which were perfect for households with small children. Today, many retrievers are "hyperactive" and can even pose a danger to children because of their unpredictability. (Of course, not all breeders are irresponsible. Dedicated hobby breeders do stop breeding a certain bloodline when they see that their animal's offspring have undesir-able genetic traits.)

Pet Stores, Puppy Mills and Backyard Breeders

10   Most dogs sold in pet stores, at auctions, through multiple breed newspaper ads, or over the Internet come from "puppy mills," where dogs are bred solely for profit. These dogs spend their entire lives in tiny cages, often with wire floors that hurt and deform their feet. Many times these cages are stacked on top of each other, so that urine and feces from animals in the top cages fall through onto the animals below. A typical mill keeps dozens of breeds and hundreds of dogs. There are also "kitten mills" where cats endure the same deplorable conditions (as well as ferret, rabbit, and rodent "mills," where these animals are produced in large numbers).

11   Dogs in puppy mills receive little, if any, veterinary care. The females are repeatedly bred, and become so fatigued from being preg-nant and delivering and caring for their pups that they no longer have the energy to clean themselves. Their coats become matted and filthy, they are depressed and malnourished, and many die young.

12   The puppies of these pitiful, neglected dogs are usually in poor health from birth. They are often abruptly weaned and sent off to pet stores when only four to six weeks old. These young pups are crammed several to a crate with little or no food or water, and shipped long distances by truck to pet stores throughout the United States. Often these pup-pies arrive at pet stores weak and sick, and many die in transit. Those that survive are sold at exorbitant prices regardless of their physical condition. Since they receive so little attention at the mill, they are poorly socialized, and many develop behavior problems, such as fear biting and house-soiling.

13   "Backyard breeders" often sell to pet stores, or by advertising in local newspapers. Backyard breeders are people who keep a few females to breed in order to sell the offspring. Although backyard breeders may breed and keep a smaller number of dogs than a puppy mill, most do it mainly for financial gain, while ignoring the overall health and disposi-tion of the dogs that they are breeding.

14   A special problem occurs with breeds that experience a burst of fame due to television or movie exposure, like Dalmatians and Jack Russell Terriers. These dogs are quickly mass-bred to take advantage of the wave of popularity, even though these breeds may not be suitable for many homes. Thousands of them will spend their lives ignored, abused, or chained in a yard, be abandoned on the street or in the countryside to die of starvation, injury, or exposure to the elements, or be sur-rendered to shelters—all because of undesir-able traits or behaviors, even though these may be quite normal for the breed.

15   Changing the way we adopt companion animals, and being more responsible about how we care for them, is the best solution.

Go On ➡

Pet Overpopulation

16   An estimated 58 million dogs and 66 million cats live in households in the United States. For every cat with a home, a cat lives homeless on the streets. Because irresponsible people—accidentally or intentionally—allow their animals to reproduce, an estimated 8–12 million dogs and cats enter shelters each year in hope of finding a permanent, loving home. However, about 55% of dogs and 76% of cats entering shelters are euthanized (killed). More than SEVEN MILLION animals are eutha-nized at shelters each year. Most of the animals killed are healthy, happy, adoptable animals. Their only crime is that they are strays, homeless, or unwanted—by-products of the serious problem of overpopulation.

17   Even if you want a special breed, always adopt rather than purchase. Twenty-five percent of animals entering shelters are purebreds, and there are many purebred rescue groups, so there is a good chance you can get the animal you want and save a life at the same time. And, of course, please, always spay and neuter your companion animals!

Our appreciation to the Animal Protection Institute for permission to use this material.

Directions for multiple-choice questions 1 through 10:	Read the passage and record your answers on the answer sheet provided.

1 Who would most likely use this article to support their position?
   A Pet store owners
   B Law enforcement officials
   C Animal shelters and adoption agencies
   D Adolescents who want a household pet

2 The author of this article would most likely agree with all of the following statements EXCEPT
   A Puppies and kittens are more adaptable than older animals.
   B Purebred animals have many health problems created by human breeders.
   C Pet overpopulation is a serious issue in our society.
   D Pet adoption is preferred over purchase of a pet.

3 In paragraph 1, why does the author cite the age range of dogs and cats?
   A To emphasize the yearly care of a pet.
   B To emphasize how long one could be responsible for a pet.
   C To emphasize that cats can live longer than dogs.
   D To emphasize that pet health problems can be costly.

4 The author says, "A special problem occurs with breeds that experience a burst of fame due to television or movie exposure." Which of the following conclusions might one draw from this statement?
   A People want breeds of pets that are "popular" at the moment.
   B Television animals are poorly socialized.
   C Television and movies that star animals are only for children.
   D Breeds that are featured in movies and television are usually neglected.

5 In paragraph 9, the word *hyperactive* is meant to contrast with which of the following?
  A temperament and behavior
  B Labrador and Golden Retrievers
  C calm and placid
  D undesirable and genetic

6 In paragraph 12, the word *exhorbitant* means
  A fair
  B excessive
  C sale
  D incredible

7 According to the author, puppy mills are guilty of all but the following:
  A Neglecting animals physically as well as emotionally.
  B Operating for profit only.
  C Confining animals to cages that are too small.
  D Breeding each animal for positive genetic traits.

8 The statement "For every cat with a home, a cat lives homeless on the streets" is an example of
  A understatement
  B hyperbole
  C contrast
  D personification

9 Which of the following would the author most likely support?
  A Development of new malls containing pet stores.
  B An Internet web site with pictures so that one could bid for pets.
  C Expenditures to develop more animal shelters in inner cities.
  D Cat and dog shows for purebred animals.

10 Which of the following BEST expresses the central idea of the article?
  A It is important to carefully research the type of pet you want before purchasing one.
  B Although they may have certain problems, purebred animals are more desirable than mixed breeds.
  C Adoption of an animal is preferable to purchase, but must be balanced with responsibility and accountability.
  D Pet overpopulation, caused by puppy mills and irresponsible breeders, has become a major concern in our society.

Go On ➡

Directions for open-ended questions 11 and 12:	Write your response in the space provided on the answer sheet.

11 A student in your class has indicated that he or she wants to purchase a breed of pet that was just featured in a popular movie.
  • Based on the article, what advice/warnings might you offer this student?
  • Provide at least two details to support this position.

Use information from the article to support your response.

12 In paragraph 3, the author says that a decision to adopt an animal should be "well informed."
  • How might you go about becoming informed about the type of animal you want?
  • What steps would you follow to become a responsible pet owner?

NJ HSPA LANGUAGE ARTS LITERACY—DAY 2
PART 5

Directions: In this part of the test, you will be asked to revise and edit text written by another student. This text will contain a variety of errors in sentence construction, usage, and mechanics. It also will present problems in content and organization. Your task is to read the text and decide what you need to do to improve it.

This section is printed to allow you to make revisions in the space between the lines of the text. If you decide to insert longer text such as sentences or paragraphs, you may use lined pages provided for your additions. As an alternate strategy, you may write the entire draft on the lined paper.

As with the writing task, you may *not* use a dictionary or any other reference materials during the test. However, you may use the Revising-Editing Guide in your booklet which explains simple ways to mark the text with your revisions and editing. It also lists the kinds of errors and writing concerns that you will need to consider as you revise and edit the text.

You will have 30 minutes for this part of the test. If you finish before the time is called, review your work to make sure that you have improved the meaning and clarity of the text.

It has always been the policy at Midway High School to require all students to take final exams in every subject. Recently, the student government association has begun to investigate the possibilities of exempting students with certain grade averages from having to take finals. One student has written an essay expressing her views on this issue. She would like to have this essay published in the school newspaper. Read the essay and think about how to improve the meaning and clarity of the text. Then make your revisions.

To the editor

I believe that final exams should be abolished for students who have had A averages in a subject for the whole year. This proves they understand the work and have studied all year. A final does not give a teacher new information about this student, I don't think.

Studying for final exams are useless if you already know the material. Besides, finals come at the end of the year when it is hot and stuffy in school. Why should an A student be penalized by having to sit for a final? When they already showed they have learned the material.

Another thing. Letting A students skip final exams would be good incentive for students to study hard all year. Especially if there is a reward at the end! Grades would probably improve for everyone if the school board dangled this "carrot" for students.

The last point I want to make is that why should one grade on one test count for so much? A final test grade is the same as a marking period grade when it is averaged into your report card which is really not fair if you had just one bad day or weren't feeling well. What a student does over the whole marking period is more important.

These are a few reasons why I think you should do away with final exams for A students. Thank you for your attention.

ANSWER KEY FOR PART 2

Multiple-Choice Questions for "Perennials"

1. **B**	Skill #1	Recognition of central idea or theme
2. **D**	Skill #11	Interpretation of textual conventions and literary elements
3. **B**	Skill #8	Prediction of tentative meanings
4. **D**	Skill #8	Prediction of tentative meanings
5. **A**	Skill #9	Forming of opinions
6. **B**	Skill #3	Extrapolation of information
	Skill #9	Forming of opinions
7. **B**	Skill #11	Interpretation of textual conventions and literary elements
8. **B**	Skill #8	Prediction of tentative meanings
9. **D**	Skill #11	Interpretation of textual conventions and literary elements
10. **C**	Skill #1	Recognition of central idea or theme
	Skill #10	Drawing conclusions

Open-Ended Responses

Use the open-ended rubric to grade your answers to questions 11 and 12. Make certain you have answered each part of the question and that you have used information from the text to support your answers.

11. Your open-ended response should address both bulleted items. The first one requires you to identify <u>two</u> ways the author has connected the narrator and ox-cart man's stories. Although there are many connections you could make between the two, the following might be included in your responses:

1. The ox-cart man and the narrator are both connected to the land on which they live. In fact, the narrator dreams that the ox-cart man returns to the narrator's farm.
2. The narrator, when imagining the ox-cart man, sees Paul's face and the face of his grandfather, thus connecting all the generations.
3. The narrator sees his purpose as the same as the ox-cart man: to create and then to divest himself of all that he has created.
4. The ox-cart man believed in the cycles of the earth, and the narrator, too, thinks that things should come full circle.
5. The narrator sees himself as a perennial and sees the ox-cart man in the same way.

Make certain to use information for the actual text to explain your answers.

The second part of your response should highlight the idea that both the narrator and the ox-cart man are perennials. A perennial is a plant that has its season, lies dormant, and then returns again in the spring. Your response should explain what the ox-cart man does every year and how he lives from season to season. In the same way, you should explain the narrator's feelings about the stories he writes; explain how he thinks it is his duty to pass stories from generation to generation, from season to season. Once again, make sure you use textual information to support your answer.

12. For this open-ended question, make sure you answer each bulleted part of the question. Your first response should speak about the writing of this short story and/or refer to the endnote from the author explaining his use of the ox-cart man's story. Remember, Paul told the narrator the story, and in retelling Paul's story, the narrator is telling the ox-cart man's story to you.

   The next part of this question calls for an individual response. You should select a story you think is particularly meaningful—perhaps something you witnessed of historical significance in your lifetime or something from your own culture, family, school, or country that you think is important. You should mention what that story might be, and why it is important that future generations hear it.

ANSWER KEY FOR PART 4

Multiple-Choice Questions for "Adopting a Companion Animal"

1. **C**	3. **B**	5. **C**	7. **D**	9. **C**
2. **A**	4. **A**	6. **B**	8. **C**	10. **C**

Open-Ended Responses

Use the open-ended rubric to grade your answers to questions 11 and 12. Make certain you have answered each part of the question and that you have used information from the text to support your answers.

11. Your open-ended response should address both bulleted items. The first bullet requires you to offer specific advice to the student in your class about buying a "popular pet." The second bullet asks that you go back to the text to provide two details to support your advice. Although there are a number of things that might be included in your response, the following may be some of the points that you make:

   1. Getting a pet is a lifelong commitment
   2. You need to get a pet that fits your lifestyle and your budget
   3. Make sure to purchase the pet from a reputable breeder
   4. Pet overpopulation is a problem, so consider adopting a pet

   Make certain to use the information from the article to explain and support your answers.

12. For this open-ended question, make sure you answer each bulleted part of the question. First, re-read paragraph number three. This discusses some ways to make a well-informed decision to buy a pet. You can also include some ideas of your own in this part of the writing. Pick up a few other ideas as stated in the article to support your answer. Refer to paragraph or line numbers if you want to quote the text.

   The second part of the question asks what steps you should follow to become a responsible pet owner. Note that it says steps, so you need to come up with more than one step. Try to think about this question sequentially; you would first research the correct pet, then buy it from a reputable seller, then care for the pet responsibly from home, and so forth. You should end your response by summing up your answer. Remember, it is always good to refer to the text to support your answer, even if it is asking for your personal opinion.

PRACTICE TEST 2
Answer Sheets

PART 1—PICTURE PROMPT WRITING TASK

Remember: This page will not be scored.

PREWRITING/PLANNING SPACE

ANSWER SHEET FOR PICTURE PROMPT WRITING TASK

ANSWER SHEET FOR PICTURE PROMPT WRITING TASK (continued)

Practice Test 2

PART 2—NARRATIVE READING

MULTIPLE-CHOICE QUESTIONS

1. Ⓐ Ⓑ Ⓒ Ⓓ   5. Ⓐ Ⓑ Ⓒ Ⓓ   8. Ⓐ Ⓑ Ⓒ Ⓓ

2. Ⓐ Ⓑ Ⓒ Ⓓ   6. Ⓐ Ⓑ Ⓒ Ⓓ   9. Ⓐ Ⓑ Ⓒ Ⓓ

3. Ⓐ Ⓑ Ⓒ Ⓓ   7. Ⓐ Ⓑ Ⓒ Ⓓ   10. Ⓐ Ⓑ Ⓒ Ⓓ

4. Ⓐ Ⓑ Ⓒ Ⓓ

11. NARRATIVE READING OPEN-ENDED RESPONSE

_____

_____

_____

_____

_____

_____

_____

_____

_____

_____

_____

_____

_____

_____

_____

_____

_____

_____

_____

_____

Practice Test 2

11. NARRATIVE READING OPEN-ENDED RESPONSE (continued)

12. NARRATIVE READING OPEN-ENDED RESPONSE

12. NARRATIVE READING OPEN-ENDED RESPONSE (continued)

PART 3—PERSUASIVE WRITING TASK

PREWRITING/PLANNING SPACE

Remember: This page will not be scored.

ANSWER SHEET FOR PERSUASIVE WRITING TASK

ANSWER SHEET FOR PERSUASIVE WRITING TASK (continued)

ANSWER SHEET FOR PERSUASIVE WRITING TASK (continued)

ANSWER SHEET FOR PERSUASIVE WRITING TASK (continued)

PART 4—PERSUASIVE READING

MULTIPLE-CHOICE QUESTIONS

1. Ⓐ Ⓑ Ⓒ Ⓓ   5. Ⓐ Ⓑ Ⓒ Ⓓ   8. Ⓐ Ⓑ Ⓒ Ⓓ

2. Ⓐ Ⓑ Ⓒ Ⓓ   6. Ⓐ Ⓑ Ⓒ Ⓓ   9. Ⓐ Ⓑ Ⓒ Ⓓ

3. Ⓐ Ⓑ Ⓒ Ⓓ   7. Ⓐ Ⓑ Ⓒ Ⓓ   10. Ⓐ Ⓑ Ⓒ Ⓓ

4. Ⓐ Ⓑ Ⓒ Ⓓ

11. PERSUASIVE READING OPEN-ENDED RESPONSE

_____

_____

_____

_____

_____

_____

_____

_____

_____

_____

_____

_____

_____

_____

_____

_____

_____

_____

_____

_____

_____

Practice Test 2

11. PERSUASIVE READING OPEN-ENDED RESPONSE (continued)

12. PERSUASIVE READING OPEN-ENDED RESPONSE

12. PERSUASIVE READING OPEN-ENDED RESPONSE (continued)

PART 5—REVISE/EDIT STUDENT TEXT

REVISE/EDIT STUDENT TEXT (continued)

WRITER'S CHECKLIST

Content/Organization

☐ 1. Your focus should be on the purpose of your writing and the audience for whom you are writing.

☐ 2. You should support your point of view with specific details and evidence.

☐ 3. The order and structure of your ideas will help communicate your view.

Sentence Construction

☐ 1. Use varied sentence structure.

☐ 2. Check that you do not have sentence fragments.

☐ 3. Check that you do not have run-on sentences.

Usage

☐ 1. Choose your words carefully so that you convey the meaning clearly.

☐ 2. Check that words have been used in the correct context.

Mechanics

☐ 1. Capitalize, spell, and punctuate correctly.

REVISING-EDITING GUIDE

You will also be given a guide with four editing conventions (things to make it easier to edit). YOU DO NOT HAVE TO USE THESE. If you have learned a different method of editing and are going to rewrite the essay on the lined paper, use this method. If you wish to use the editing marks from the editing guide, then practice using them in your own first drafts so that you do not have to think about them:

1.

   The words in the circle are the words you want to move. The arrow shows you where to move these words.

2. ~~Cross out~~
   shows that you want to completely get rid of these words.

3. ^ shows that you want to insert a word or several words. You write the words or word above the ^.

4. Ⓐ tells the reader to go to the section you have labeled *A* and read that text, then to return to this text.

You are doing exactly what you do when you peer edit and revise in your classes, so you have had a lot of practice at this.

PRACTICE TEST 2

NJ HSPA LANGUAGE ARTS LITERACY—DAY 1
PART 1

Directions:	Today you are going to take part of the High School Proficiency Assessment for Language Arts Literacy. The assessment contains different types of text and different activities. In the first part of the test, you will look at a picture and then complete a writing task. In this activity, you have an opportunity to demonstrate how well you can organize and express your ideas in written text. Refer to the Writer's Checklist of important points to remember as you write. Educators who read your writing will consider these important points when they read and score your writing.

Directions: Today you are going to take part of the High School Proficiency Assessment for Language Arts Literacy. The assessment contains different types of text and different activities. In the first part of the test, you will look at a picture and then complete a writing task. In this activity, you have an opportunity to demonstrate how well you can organize and express your ideas in written text. Refer to the Writer's Checklist of important points to remember as you write. Educators who read your writing will consider these important points when they read and score your writing.

You will have 30 minutes to complete the writing task. Take a few minutes to think about the task and to plan what you want to say before you begin to write. You may use the prewriting/planning space to plan your text, but your prewriting will not be scored. **Only your writing on the lined pages of your answer sheet will be scored.** Do your best to make your writing clear and well organized. Keep your purpose in mind as you write and use your checklist.

You must use a No. 2 pencil. You may either print or write your final copy. You may *not* use a dictionary or any other reference materials during the test. However, you may use the Writer's Checklist. If you finish before the time is called, review what you have written using the Writer's Checklist to read critically and improve what you have written.

Practice Test 2

Credit: bigfoto.com

An ancient proverb says, "A picture is worth a thousand words." Regardless of the artist's original intent, what we see in the picture can be very different from what others see. What story does this picture tell you? Use your imagination and experience to speculate about what is happening. Then write your story.

NJ HSPA LANGUAGE ARTS LITERACY—DAY 1
PART 2

Directions: In this part of the test, you will read a narrative passage and then respond to the multiple-choice and open-ended questions that follow it. You may look back at the passage and make notes in the margin if you like, but you must record your answers on your answer sheet.

You will have 50 minutes for this part of the test.

The following excerpt comes from *Journey to the Golden Door: A Survivor's Tale* by Jay Sommer. Mr. Sommer was the 1981 National Teacher of the Year and today is a professor at Fairfield University in Fairfield, Connecticut. The autobiography from which this excerpt is taken relates the author's extraordinary experiences as a child, adolescent, and young adult during World War II, including his escape from a Nazi labor camp and his involuntary service in the Soviet Army.

The following passage takes place around 1944, after Hitler has occupied Hungary. The author has been working in a labor camp from which he has just escaped. He must obtain false papers to hide his identity and find work to sustain him. He returns to Budapest, to an old print shop with which he is familiar. From *Journey to the Golden Door* by Jay Sommer:

1   My new identity well memorized, I emerged apprehensively from my crawl space ready to go to the printing shop. I carried a small bundle containing a threadbare sweater, a shirt, a pair of socks, and briefs. It was a brilliantly sunny August day. Having been confined to almost total darkness for a whole week, I had to squint for a long time before I could fully open my eyes. Among the crowds milling about the streets were large numbers of German SS walking in pairs, and my heart pounded every time I passed them. I felt totally isolated, a terrified being, an alien walking among the people leading a normal life, Hungarian men and women strolled along as happily as they had before Hitler had come to Hungary only five months earlier. Perhaps some of them didn't know, or didn't care that just a few streets away there was a large synagogue into which hundreds of Jewish men, women, and children had been crammed before being sent to Auschwitz.

2   The printing shop was situated in a basement. Ferenc recognized me when I entered, and said in a loud voice, "Hello, Micky [my Hungarian name], what are you doing here?" His words sounded to me more like an accusation than a welcome. "Aren't you supposed to be in some camp or other?" he asked in the same unfriendly tone. I was glad he was alone so that I could come to the point very quickly and explain the reason for my visit. He suddenly became restless and abrupt. Saying he was very busy, he asked what name and age I wanted on the identification papers. Unwise as it sounds, I felt I had no choice but to trust him despite his hostile reception. He told me to come back the following morning, but I left feeling pretty doubtful about whether he would indeed have the documents for me.

3   It was almost noon when I came out of the printing shop. I started walking very quickly, looking back several times to see if I was being followed. I went to a nearby park, consumed my last bit of salami and bread, and washed it down with fresh water from a fountain. Not knowing what else to do, I walked aimlessly through the streets of Budapest until an impulse propelled me in the direction of the shop where I had worked in what now seemed another lifetime. It was as though I wanted to believe that everything was all right, that I was still a working mechanic rather than a fugitive in grave danger.

Go On ➡

Across the street from the shop, I found a spot from which I could see one of my former colleagues working with a welding torch, my favorite job. At the large office window, I saw Mr. Szecsenyi sitting in the chair where the Jewish owner, Mr. Feifer, used to sit. The store had apparently been confiscated, and Mr. Feifer was now most likely waiting in the ghetto or already at Auschwitz.

4   After spending an hour watching the activities of the shop in which I would have loved to be working, I left and continued wandering the streets. Exhausted and hungry, I began to think of where I could safely spend the night. All sorts of possibilities ran through my mind, most of them impractical or dangerous. I thought of hiding in the sewers, something I had seen in a movie about Paris, but then I thought of the rats that would be there and immediately abandoned that idea. I also thought of locking myself in one of the underground toilets, but that didn't appear safe enough. I decided my best bet was to try the place where I had been living at the time of my departure for labor camp. My landlady who had appeared sympathetic and even seemed upset when I was summoned to Jolsva would perhaps allow me to stay over for one night. It was already dusk when I got there. I had to be sure that neither Szecsenyi nor his wife, the concierge, would see me, for that would definitely spell trouble.

5   I succeeded in getting to the third floor, where my former landlady occupied a three-bedroom apartment, without being noticed by any of the neighbors who might have recognized me. At the sight of me, the landlady exclaimed, "Jesus Maria, you are alive?" I could tell from her face that she was quite taken aback by my appearance—it hadn't occurred to me that my recent experiences had wrought such great changes. As I had with Ferenc, I gave her a brief account of my situation, but unlike his unresponsive reaction, hers was compassionate; she even wept as I spoke. She offered me food, which I gobbled up gratefully and in great haste, as had become my habit, as if it might be taken from me before I finished it all.

6   As to whether I could stay overnight with her, she was very reluctant and even afraid to give me an answer; she said she would let me know if Mr. Szecsenyi agreed to it. As far as I could see, this reduced my chances to zero. I

could only pray that this hateful man had mellowed in the five months since he had last seen me. It didn't take long, though, to find out I was mistaken. As soon as he saw me, he flew into a rage, screaming anti-Semitic insults. The dumbfounded landlady never had a chance to finish her plea on my behalf. Mr. Szecsenyi obviously understood right away what it was all about and made it quite plain that if I didn't clear out immediately he would denounce me to the authorities.

7   It was already around ten o'clock, a dangerous time for a luckless Jewish escapee to be in the city without identification. As I was leaving the building, I noticed an open window that led to the basement. Whoever had left it that way would never know what a blessed favor he had done me. I climbed through and found myself in a dark boiler room that was not only pleasantly warm but even had a spot where I could sleep fairly comfortably. It was certainly an improvement on the damp crawl space in Imre's building and preferable to sleeping in the sewers with the rats. Fortunately, though the basement also served as an air raid shelter, no one had reason to come down there that night. Even if they had, my refuge was so well-concealed that only a bloodhound would have found me. Considering Mr. Szecsenyi's outbursts and threats to report me, the boiler room might not have seemed the safest place to spend the night, but my choice turned out to be a good one after all. Having found some torn blankets, I was able to fix up a cozy sleeping place—better than the wooden cot in the tool shed at Bukavinka and the pile of straw at Jolsva.

8   Since I was physically exhausted and emotionally drained, sleep came easily that night. As if to reassure me, Providence sent my mother in a dream. I had not dreamed of her in a long time. She was covering me with the little patched blanket that she had made for me when I went away to cheder [school], and she whispered softly her oft-repeated words of comfort, "Zorg zich nisht, Gott it unz helfen [Don't worry the Almighty will help us]." When I awoke in the morning, I heard myself repeating Mother's soothing words.

9   The tolling of the church bells across the street informed me that it was eight o'clock. I was sure that Mr. Szecsenyi had left the house by now. Since climbing out of the window might arouse suspicion, I waited for the right moment

to leave through the gates. As I made my way to the printing shop, I passed several sidewalk cafes. It was painful to see people eating huge breakfasts while I was terribly hungry. But without a penny to my name, all I could do was pray that I would get my new identity document and find a job quickly. Despite my empty stomach I walked briskly, again looking constantly over my shoulder in fear that someone might be following me. At the printer's, I was careful not to go right down to the basement, but passed it a few times to make sure Ferenc was alone. Just when I thought it was safe, and was about to go in, I took one more look and was horrified to see two German soldiers with rifles on their shoulders speaking to my supposed benefactor. I did what any frightened fugitive would do—turned around and ran for dear life as far as my breath and my legs would permit. When I no longer had the strength to run, I sat down on a bench in a small park a good distance away. Feeling safe for the moment, I was able to recover my equilibrium. I have no way of knowing for sure that Ferenc had betrayed me, but I strongly suspect that the Germans were waiting for me and that this had been a close call.

Thanks to Mr. Jay Sommer for permission to use this excerpt.

Directions for multiple-choice questions 1 through 10:	Read the passage and record your answers on the answer sheet provided.

1 The reader infers that the narrator needed new identification papers because

 A he had lost his original ones.

 B he wanted to assume a new identity.

 C he needed them to get a driver's license.

 D he wanted to give the printer work to do.

2 The narrator considers all of the following places to hide for the night except

 A the underground toilets.

 B the sewers under the streets.

 C his landlady's apartment.

 D the printer's shop.

3 In paragraph 5, the phrase *taken aback* is closest in meaning to

 A surprised

 B angry

 C amused

 D reminded

4 When Mr. Szecsenyi tells the narrator he will "denounce" him to the authorities, he means

 A he will find him government housing.

 B he will report him to the government.

 C he will wrestle him to the ground.

 D he will complain to the government.

5 The reader infers that the reason the narrator has no money is because

 A the printer refused to pay him.

 B Mr. Szecsenyi called the police rather than pay him.

 C he lost his job when the Nazis occupied his country.

 D he lost his money running away from the police.

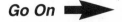
Go On

6 The tone of the passage is
  A objective
  B whining
  C pompous
  D didactic

7 In paragraph 9, the phrase *recover my equilibrium* means
  A almost fell and regained his balance.
  B regained his composure.
  C fell asleep on the bench.
  D found his lost money.

8 The reader can infer from this excerpt that
  A Ferenc was a Nazi sympathizer.
  B his landlady called the authorities.
  C the narrator was paranoid.
  D the German soldiers were sympathetic to the narrator.

9 In paragraph 8, what does the author mean by "Providence sent my mother"?
  A Providence was his landlady's name.
  B His mother's image appeared to him when he most needed her.
  C Providence was an agency that helped reunite children and their parents.
  D Providence is where he originally lived.

10 We can infer from the passage that the narrator was
  A a Jewish man persecuted by the Nazis.
  B a Nazi sympathizer living in Hungary.
  C an American soldier during World War II.
  D educated in Budapest.

Directions for open-ended questions 11 and 12:	Write your response in the space provided on the answer sheet.

11 The author of this passage reports some of the steps that he had to take in order to survive during World War II.
  • Which of his efforts at survival do you think were the most difficult?
  • Why do you think this was the most difficult?

12 In paragraph 9, the author relates how he was betrayed to the authorities.
  • Do you think that his suspicion that Ferenc betrayed him is logical?
  • Which details in the passage support your conclusion?

NJ HSPA LANGUAGE ARTS LITERACY—DAY 2
PART 3

Directions: In this part of the test, you will complete a persuasive writing task. You will have an opportunity to demonstrate how well you can organize and express your ideas in written text. Refer to the Writer's Checklist of important points to remember as you write. Educators who read your writing will consider these important points when they read and score your writing.

You will have 60 minutes to complete this writing task. Take a few minutes to think about the task and to plan what you want to say before you begin to write. You may use the prewriting/planning space to plan your text, but your prewriting will not be scored. Do your best to make your writing clear and well organized. Keep your audience and purpose in mind as you write and use your checklist.

You must use a No. 2 pencil. You may either print or write your final copy. You may *not* use a dictionary or any other reference materials during the test. However, you may use the Writer's Checklist. If you finish before the time is called, review what you have written, using the Writer's Checklist to read critically and improve what you have written.

WRITING SITUATION

Your community is being asked to consolidate its high school system with a neighboring community's school system. Although the two communities are next to each other, they are very different in the makeup of their population. The proponents of this plan argue that this merger will provide more opportunities for all students. The opponents of the plan believe that merging the two high schools will create too many problems.

WRITING TASK

Write an editorial for the local newspaper expressing your views on this proposal. The purpose is to persuade the reader that your viewpoint should be adopted. Assume that you are discussing your own community and a neighboring community. Support your position with reasons, examples, facts, and/or other evidence.

NJ HSPA LANGUAGE ARTS LITERACY—DAY 2
PART 4

Practice Test 2

Directions: In this part of the test, you will read a narrative passage and then respond to the multiple-choice and open-ended questions that follow it. You may look back at the passage and make notes in the margin if you like, but you must record your answers on your answer sheet.

You will have 45 minutes for this part of the test.

Home Aquariums
Monica Engebretson

From <u>Animal Issues</u>. Volume 32 Number 3, Fall 2001
Reprinted by permission of the Animal Protection Institute

1   Often described as "living art," home aquariums are beautiful and fascinating, offering us a window into another world from the comfort and convenience of our home . . . but at what cost to the environment and the fish?

2   More than 90 million tropical fish are purchased for aquariums each year around the world—an estimated $100 million trade. Two-thirds of the world's 1.5 million aquarium hobbyists are Americans who, according to the U.S. Coral Reef Task Force's committee on international trade, buy half of the aquarium fish and up to 80% of the coral traded in the world. The next largest importers are Germany and Japan. Benign as aquariums may seem, the international trade in corals and fish is driving destructive and unsustainable collection practices that are wreaking havoc on tropical marine ecosystems.

3   Coral reefs are the oldest, most complex ecosystems in the ocean—the marine equivalent of tropical rainforests in terms of ecosystem diversity and productivity. All over the world, entire coral reef ecosystems are collapsing at unprecedented rates. Current techniques used to capture fish for the aquarium market, including the use of explosives and poisons, can severely damage coral reefs.

4   The demand for tropical fish to fill aquariums has fueled the trade in illegal fish collection in which divers squirt cyanide into reefs to stun fish, polluting the environment and killing smaller fish and coral. According to the International Marinelife Alliance, more countries in the world use nets rather than cyanide to capture fish, but two of the biggest exporters, Indonesia and the Philippines, collect more than half of their aquarium fish with cyanide despite local laws prohibiting the practice.

5   Aquarium hobbyists also impact coral reefs by buying up live coral. The U.S. bans harvesting of coral in its own waters, so most of the supply comes from loosely protected reefs in poorer countries. Coral reefs in Southeast Asia are severely threatened or degraded due to many factors, including the use of cyanide explosives to catch fish and international trade in coral. The 1998 Reefs at Risk report by the World Resources Institute found that more than 80% of the reefs in this region are at risk from human activities.

6   Not only poor countries are losing their reefs. Almost no regulations control the coral trade in Japan. Various types of live coral from Japan's coastal areas, including rare species, are sold in pet shops in and around Tokyo. In Australia, licensed operators harvested 50 tons of coral from the Great Barrier Reef in 2000. However, in June 2001, Australia's Environmental Minister said he would discuss a phase-out of commercial coral harvesting on the reef.

7   All marine "salt water" species seen in home aquariums are wild-caught. Each year, 70 to 100 tons of wild marine fish are captured for the aquarium trade. Not surprisingly, many exploited species are on the decline (see "Seahorses" below). Hawaii's 1998 State of the Reefs Report stated that in a 20-year period the 10 species most collected in Hawaii for the aquarium trade declined by 59%.

8   Many freshwater species are also wild-caught. There are more than 1,000 species of freshwater fish in Southeast Asia. Much of the "official" trade has been with farm-bred species such as guppies, goldfishes, koi, mollies, swordtails, and cichlids, none of which are native to the region. While the nonprofit Ornamental Fish International claims that 90% of freshwater fish exported from Singapore are bred in captivity, the National University of Singapore suspects that a substantial part of the trade includes wild-caught fish that have been labeled, "bred in captivity." According to the University, for most species captive breeding is simply not economical; it is far cheaper to catch wild fish.

9   The environmental threats of home aquariums do not end with the removal of fish from their native environments. The release of exotic fish by well-intentioned or disenchanted aquarium hobbyists into the nearest body of water creates problems for native fish and the ecosystem in general.

10   If exotic fish survive and reproduce, their presence may lead to changes in the native fish population through competition for resources or by preying on them. Introduced fish may also infect native fish with exotic parasites or diseases, and aquarium fish may affect the genetics of native species by hybridizing with them.

11   Currently, at least 185 different species of exotic fishes have been caught in open waters of the United States, and 75 of these are known to have established breeding populations. More than half of these introductions are due to the release or escape of aquarium fish. Because many of the released fish are native to tropical regions of the world, most introduced fish in the U.S. have become established in Florida, Texas, and the Southwest.

12   Environmental concerns aside, are there other ethical implications of keeping fish in aquariums? Are aquarium fish aware of their captivity? Do they suffer from being deprived of their natural environment or ability to express behaviors that have evolved in them over hundreds of millions of years? As some aquarium enthusiasts point out, fish placed in a suitable aquatic environment are much closer to their natural habitat than many animals held in zoo enclosures or birds kept in cages, as if this were sufficient justification to keep fish. Since most fish are used to swimming in large open spaces with freedom of movement, the only truly "suitable aquatic environment" would be their natural habitat.

13   As with all animals we cannot know for sure what a fish is thinking or even if he or she is thinking. But, just like cat and dog guardians, many aquarium owners will attest that their fish have personalities, communicate their desires, and "play" with their human caretakers. A recent study on pain in fish confirms that indeed fish have conscious, cognizant pain experiences similar to higher vertebrates such as mammals. If fish are similar to other animals in their ability to feel pain, then it is not unreasonable to assume that they share other sensations such as fear, joy, and sadness. In lieu of definitive answers to the emotional lives of fish and in consideration of the negative impacts the aquarium trade has on wild fish populations and the environment, we should admire fish in their natural habitats, not in our homes.

14   Seahorses are at once beautiful, graceful, and odd. Not only do these fish look strange—like tiny horses with monkey tails—their behavior and biology is fascinating. Seahorses mate for life (when a partner is lost it is unlikely that the remaining mate will find a new partner), and it is the male who gets pregnant, carries the young in a kangaroo-like pouch, goes through saber, and gives birth. Alas, the seahorse's mystique is leading to its demise.

15   Global seahorse populations have declined dramatically in recent years—as much as 50% in some areas in a 5- to 10-year period. In Chinese medicine the seahorses' fidelity has come to be equated with sexual health. Pound for pound, dead, dried and bleached seahorses are more valuable than silver on the Hong Kong market, where they are used for a variety of Chinese treatments. While collection for Chinese medicine and habitat loss probably

Go On ➡

represent the largest threat to seahorses, thousands of wild seahorses are collected for the aquarium trade. Twenty countries, including the United States, export seahorses for aquariums and to be used in folk medicines.

16   It is a common misconception that buying seahorses for home aquariums or attempting to rear them in captivity will help conservation efforts. In fact, buying seahorses contributes to the decline of wild populations. Almost all seahorses sold by marine retailers are wild-caught rather than captive-bred, because raising seahorses to maturity is difficult and it is more profitable to collect them from the wild. Despite numerous claims of successful breeding and rearing in some species of seahorses, there is a lack of rigorous scientific publications to substantiate the claims. The few "captive-reared" seahorses are usually the young of wild-caught pregnant males. Seahorses are extremely difficult to maintain in home aquariums and most hobbyists end up replacing their lost seahorses frequently, thus perpetuating the trade.

17   Siamese fighting fish (Betta splendens), called "bettas," are commonly sold in pet shops, retail stores, and at fairs. Natives of Southeast Asia, most bettas are "cultured" (bred in captivity) in their native homelands and exported to the U.S. where they are frequently sold in tiny barren bowls and are treated more like home and office accessories than living, feeling beings.

18   People often purchase these and other fish such as goldfish on impulse, especially when sold in retail stores like Wal-Mart or given as prizes at local fairs. Typically, people do not enter retail stores or attend fairs intending to acquire something that will require daily care, and often are not adequately informed about the special care required for fish. In order to thrive, fish require good quality dechlorinated water, sufficient water surface, correct water temperature, a balance of light and darkness, appropriate habitat, and a proper diet. The small barren containers such as plastic cups are clearly inappropriate. Such containers do not provide adequate surface area, swimming space, or environmental enrichment (plants, rocks, etc.) that would at least mimic the animals' natural environment.

19   You can help. If you see fish for sale in retail stores or local gifts shops, or offered as prizes at a local fair, let the owner or manager of the store or the fair organizer know that treating animals like merchandise is unacceptable.

Directions for multiple-choice questions 1 through 10:	Read the passage and record your answers on the answer sheet provided.

1 The structure of this essay moves from
   A a question, to support, to a call for action.
   B statistics, to examples, to personal experience.
   C examples, to accusations, to personal observation.
   D personal experience, to examples, to accusations.

2 Paragraph 2 infers that
   A Germany and Japan are to blame for coral reef destruction.
   B American hobbyists are to blame for supporting the fish hobby industry.
   C marine ecosystems in the tropics are supported by Americans.
   D Germany and Japan are competing with America in the fish hobby industry.

3 The author of this article names two major factors that are destroying coral reefs. They
   are
   A cyanide explosives used to catch fish and the international trading of coral.
   B poor countries opening too many pet stores.
   C local laws prohibiting the sale of coral.
   D fish eating the coral at an alarming rate.

4 In paragraph 9, *disenchanted* means
   A magical
   B angry
   C disillusioned
   D disgusted

5 In paragraph 18, the author is implying <u>all</u> but the following:
   A Retail stores are not as good as pet stores for buying fish.
   B Impulse buying of fish results in people not caring for them very well.
   C Fish care is a lot more complicated than most people imagine.
   D Small containers do not show off the fish well enough.

6 In paragraph 16 the author says, "Almost all seahorses sold by marine retailers are
   wild-caught rather than captive-bred."
   A This supports the idea that too many seahorses are caught in the wild.
   B This supports the idea that a home aquarium is no place to keep a seahorse.
   C This supports the idea that China exports too many seahorses.
   D This supports the idea that people can successfully breed seahorses.

7 In paragraph 16, the word *perpetuating* means
   A ceasing
   B continuing
   C forcing
   D increasing

8 Why does the author claim that "it is far cheaper to catch wild fish"?
   A Fishermen are not paid that much.
   B It takes too many resources to trap fish.
   C It takes too long and costs too much to breed fish in captivity.
   D There are so many fish in the wild, it is easier to net them than trap them.

9 In paragraph 2, *wreaking havoc* most nearly means
   A creating order
   B creating chaos
   C bringing pleasure
   D illegally exploring

10 Releasing exotic fish into new environments can have all but the following effects:
    A Native fish can become infected with parasites.
    B Exotic fish will compete with native fish for available food.
    C Exotic fish will miss their old environments.
    D Exotic fish may breed with native fish.

Practice Test 2

Go On ➡

Directions for open-ended questions 11 and 12:	Write your response in the space provided on the answer sheet.

11 In paragraph 12, the author discusses some ethical implications of keeping fish in aquariums.
  • If the author were a guest speaker in your science class, what two questions might you ask her about aquarium fish?
  • How might these answers change your views about fish?

Use information from the article to support your response.

12 In paragraph 13, the author discusses a recent study on pain sensations in fish.
  • Do you believe this is a strong argument that supports her position?
  • Which of the author's arguments are most convincing to you?

NJ HSPA LANGUAGE ARTS LITERACY—DAY 2
PART 5

Directions: In this part of the test, you will be asked to revise and edit text written by another student. This text will contain a variety of errors in sentence construction, usage, and mechanics. It also will present problems in content and organization. Your task is to read the text and decide what you need to do to improve it.

This section is printed to allow you to make revisions in the space between the lines of the text. If you decide to insert longer text such as sentences or paragraphs, you may use lined pages provided for your additions. As an alternate strategy, you may write the entire draft on the lined paper.

As with the writing task, you may *not* use a dictionary or any other reference materials during the test. However, you may use the Revising-Editing Guide, which explains simple ways to mark the text with your revisions and editing. It also lists the kinds of errors and writing concerns that you will need to consider as you revise and edit the text.

You will have 30 minutes for this part of the test. If you finish before the time is called, review your work to make sure that you have improved the meaning and clarity of the text.

Students have been reading about cloning in their science classes. Their English teacher has given them several articles to read by different authors, some of whom are in favor of cloning human beings, and some of whom are against it. Students have been asked to write a brief essay expressing their personal opinion regarding the cloning of human beings.

Revise the following essay, written by one of the students:

In the 21'st century it will probably be possible to clone human beings although whether we want to do that remain a ethical question which has still to be satisfactorily solved.

The first issue is whether we as a society have any control over whether scientists will clone people. We can refuse to allow governmental money to be used for this type of research to use human beings as guinea pigs. But can we control the use of many government money worldwide. This would have taken a worldwide effort and a possible relinquishing of civil liberties. So therefore if the population cant control the research do we really have any choice in the matter.

If we want the ability to make morally decisions regarding this research and cloning human beings than we need to first figure out how to control scientific research and inquiry.

Therefore I believe that the issue is not whether we should or should not clone human beings but whether we can do anything to stop others from doing so. Until we address these questions we cannot even begin to deal with the ethical issues involved in this matter.

ANSWER KEY FOR PART 2

Multiple-Choice Questions for "Journey to the Golden Door: A Survivor's Tale" excerpt

1. **A** B   3. **A**   5. **D**   7. **B**   9. **B**
2. **B** D   4. **C** B   6. **A**   8. **C**   10. **C** A

Oen-ended Responses

Use the open-ended rubric to grade your answers to questions 11 and 12. Make certain you have answered each part of the question and that you have used information from the text to support your answers.

11. Once again, there are two bulleted questions that need to be answered in this question. The first asks you to first consider the steps the author took to survive the war. These are in the story. Now, it asks that you decide which of these steps were the most difficult. You need to select at least two steps, since this is what the question is asking of you. After you identify at least two steps, you must explain why you think they were the most difficult.

Any of the following might be one or more of the "steps" you identified as being some of the most difficult the author had to face for survival:

1. The author had to seek help in finding new identity papers.
2. The author had to find shelter by trusting a relative stranger.
3. The author crawled into a basement to find shelter.
4. The author must often go hungry and wander the streets that are unsafe.

You might identify any of these steps as some of the more difficult for the author. You next are asked to explain your answer. This means explaining why the two steps you choose to identify were the most difficult for the author. Do not forget to go back into the text to support your answer.

12. This question refers to a specific paragraph – paragraph number 9. Go back and re-read this paragraph thoroughly. You are being asked for your opinion, based on the reading. You should be specific by saying that you agree or disagree with the author's assessment that Ferenc betrayed him. After making up your mind about the answer, the next bullet asks that you go back to the paragraph and identify the specific details that support your answer.

If you state that you agree with the author that Ferenc betrayed him, you might point out the following details:

1. Ferenc was originally acting suspicious when first asked to obtain the false papers.
2. Ferenc was speaking to two German soldiers in his shop.
3. Ferenc was unfriendly to the author from the very beginning.

If you state that you do not agree that Ferenc betrayed the author, you will need to state some other textual proofs such as:

1. The author cannot know if the German soldiers were summoned by Ferenc or not.
2. Ferenc may have just been afraid of helping the author and therefore seemed unfriendly.

ANSWER KEY FOR PART 4

Multiple-Choice Questions for "Home Aquariums"

1. **B**	3. **A**	5. **C**	7. **B**	9. **B**
2. **D**	4. **B**	6. **A**	8. **A**	10. **A**

Open-ended Responses

Use the open-ended rubric to grade your answers to questions 11 and 12. Make certain you have answered each part of the question and that you have used information from the text to support your answers.

11. For this question, you are first directed to a specific paragraph in the reading. In this case, you need to focus your attention and answer on paragraph number 12. You are also asked to think about the ethical implications of keeping fish in aquariums as explained by the author. For the first part of your response, you need to think of two questions you would ask her if given the opportunity. You must think of two questions; one will not give you full credit on this answer!

    After explaining the two questions you might ask the author, you are now asked to complete your response by saying how the anwers to your questions could change your thoughts about aquarium fish.

    1. For example, if you were to ask the author if fish are "aware of their captivity" and the author said "yes," how would that change the way you think about fish in captivity?
    2. If you asked the author if fish in aquariums suffered and the author said "yes," in what way would you change your thinking?

12. Once again, for this question you are referred to a specific place in the text. In this case, you need to re-read paragraph number 13. This paragraph discusses pain sensations in fish. The first bullet of this question asks if you believe that this particular argument strongly supports the author's position. You must decide how you feel about the strength of the "pain" argument and make a statement about your belief. The next bullet asks that you evaluate the author's other arguments and decide which ones are the most convincing to you.

    Your response might highlight any of these arguments used by the author:

    1. Fish may feel pain.
    2. Fish may be aware of being in aquariums.
    3. People are not prepared to take good care of their fish.
    4. Capturing fish may damage coral reefs and other ecosystems.
    5. Fish may have sensations like joy, fear, or sadness.
    6. Wild fish populations make their populations decline.

    Remember, you need to tell why these arguments are convincing to you in order to receive full credit for your answer.

Appendices

APPENDIX A: NEW JERSEY CORE CURRICULUM CONTENT STANDARDS FOR LANGUAGE ARTS LITERACY

The New Jersey Core Curriculum Content Standards were first adopted by the State Board of Education in 1996. These standards describe what students should know, understand, and be able to do from kindergarten through graduation from high school. The standards in New Jersey are revised every 5 years, and provide each district with a roadmap in every discipline for what students need to accomplish year by year.

The New Jersey Core Curriculum Content Standards for Language Arts Literacy are the standards specific to English/Language Arts instruction. The Language Arts Standards consist of five specific areas that are intended to build students' literacy skills in order that they become life-long learners and thinkers. The five Language Arts standards are: Reading, Writing, Speaking, Listening, and Viewing and Media Literacy. Each standard is numbered—3.1 through 3.5. Each of these five areas is then subdivided into specific skills and knowledge (known as Cumulative Progress Indicators) that students need to know at every grade level of their education.

What follows are the Language Arts standards for grades nine through twelve. Essentially, they show the skills and knowledge for which all students in New Jersey should be accountable throughout high school. These are the most recent grades 9–12 standards that were revised as of January 2008. If you are interested in seeing the Language Arts standards for grades K–8, you can visit the New Jersey Department of Education website at: http://www.nj.gov/. At this site, click on **Education** and you can follow the links to view all of the standards for every discipline, including Language Arts.

INTRODUCTION

The Vision

The New Jersey Core Curriculum Content Standards for Language Arts Literacy capture language experiences all children need in order to grow intellectually, socially, and emotionally in classrooms across the curriculum. The standards are intended to promote students' capacities to construct meaning in any arena, with others as well as on their own. If students learn to read, write, speak, listen, and view critically, strategically, and creatively, and if they learn to use these arts individually and with others, they will have the literacy skills they need to discover personal and shared meaning throughout their lives.

The language arts are integrative, interactive ways of communicating that develop through reading, writing, speaking, listening, and viewing. They are the means through which one is able to receive information; think logically and creatively; express ideas; understand and participate meaningfully in spoken, written, and nonverbal communications; formulate and answer questions; and search for, organize, evaluate, and apply information. Literacy is a way to acquire knowledge for thinking and communicating; it is more than the acquisition of a specific, predetermined set of skills in reading, writing, speaking, listening, and viewing. Literacy is also recognizing and understanding one's own purposes for thinking and communicating (through print or nonprint, verbal or nonverbal means) and being able to use one's own resources to achieve those purposes.

Underlying the standards for Language Arts Literacy are four assumptions about language learning. First, language is an active process for constructing meaning. Even the quiet listener is actively working to link prior knowledge and understanding to what other people say. Second, language develops in a social context. While language is used in private activities, the use of language almost always relates to others. Each of us is an active audience for those who create spoken, written, or visual texts; others listen to our thoughts as they read our writing. Third, language ability increases in complexity if language is used in increasingly complex ways. Language learners must engage in texts and conversations that are rich in ideas and increasingly complex in the patterns of language they display. Finally, learners achieve mastery of language arts literacy not by adding skills one-by-one to their repertoire, but rather by using and exploring language in its many dimensions.

Although the standards define five separate strands of the language arts, these arts are integrative and meant to work together to inform and enrich each other. The language arts are interdependent processes that often merge in an integrated act of rehearsal, reflection, and learning. The division of language arts into separate standards and lettered strands is merely a method that allows us to highlight the special features of each and to identify developmentally appropriate skills and behaviors among language arts learners. The separation is not meant to suggest hierarchical order or any linear or sequential approach to literacy instruction. The standards are not intended to be a curriculum guide but should be used as a catalyst for curriculum alignment and renewal. They are the foundation for the universal thinking skills and strategies that enable all learners to contribute effectively to a global society.

The standards represent the importance of language arts to learning in two distinct but complementary ways. On the one hand, students develop the skills they will carry with them into adulthood as contributing members of society: critical thinking, problem solving, and creativity. On the other hand, students discover the inner joy and self-illumination that come with reading great literature and communicating through speech and writing. These two views are complementary; in striving for the goals of one, the goals of the other are fostered.

State Reading Goal

A primary state goal for reading, and cornerstone of the recent education reform initiative, is that **"Students will read well and independently by the end of the third grade."** In order to accomplish this goal, the language arts committee has placed a strong emphasis on developing performance benchmarks in grades K–12 that reflect both a state and national perspective on reading achievement. Teachers and parents can assist students in achieving these proficiencies by recognizing that learning extends beyond the classroom door to everyday experiences related to self, others, and the world.

The following set of beliefs about students, teaching, and the language arts learning process were established as the underlying framework for standards revisions. A "balanced and comprehensive approach" to instruction is essential in all language arts programs, and classrooms should provide students with:

• Differentiated instructional strategies to address individual learning styles and diverse student needs;
• Exposure to and experience with many literary genres through reaction, reflection, and introspection;

- Instructional skills and strategies, including direct and explicit instruction; modeling of skills/strategies for students, and opportunities for students to be a teacher to others, that ready students to become competent readers, writers, speakers, listeners, and viewers;
- Instruction delivered in meaningful contexts so that students preserve the learning for future use or transfer to other learning;
- "Active learning" in which students are engaged in active questioning, active listening, authentic activities, and the learning process;
- Explicit teaching of skills as a means of supporting mastery of standard English conventions, comprehension strategies, and communication skills;
- Acquisition of reading and literacy skills in all content areas to support learning;
- Development of self-help strategies that are practiced across all disciplines;
- Connections to prior knowledge as a necessary component of new learning and retention;
- Immersion in reading, writing, listening, speaking, and viewing strands that leads to deeper and wider understanding;
- Use of textual resources, especially those linked to current technologies, as an integral part of a language arts literacy program;
- Experiences using technology as a tool for learning, especially as it applies to research and data retrieval;
- Time to practice learned skills and reflect on one's work as an important part of the learning process;
- Activities encouraging problem-solving and inquiry skills as critical attributes to learning; and
- Explicit and systematic instruction in phonics and phonemic awareness, fluency, comprehension, and vocabulary development.

The language arts classroom should be purposeful, stimulating to the senses, and engaging for all types of learners, including varied activities for visual, auditory, and kinesthetic learners. Classroom organization should include some form of team and partner work and provide an environment that is responsive to students' personal and academic goals.

Brain-based research clearly shows implications for student learning when there are links to the arts, like classical music, and the real world. For example, having young children recite the alphabet with a song enables the learner to remember and retain the information longer. Language arts classrooms should be alive with authentic learning opportunities that motivate and incorporate the arts.

Revised Standards

The language arts standards adopted by the State Board of Education in 1996 and the revised standards continue to be aligned with national standards developed by the National Council of Teachers of English and the International Reading Association. Achieve, Inc., reviewed New Jersey's 1996 standards in language arts literacy and provided recommendations for improvement. They suggested that the standards provide more clarity and specificity by including benchmarking at more grade levels. In addition, New Jersey standards should reflect sufficient rigor and complexity from grade level to grade level. Achieve recommended that attention be given to the primary grades and integration of phonics instruction in the context of meaningful reading and writing tasks. Achieve's recommendations are reflected in the revised standards.

The revised standards are also influenced by the research of the National Reading Panel (2000). There are five dimensions in early reading, plus a child's motivation to read, that must be developed so that young students become proficient readers. A comprehensive and balanced elementary literacy program should include the following areas:

• Phonemic awareness;
• Explicit and systematic phonics;
• Reading fluency;
• Reading comprehension;
• Vocabulary development; and
• Individual child's motivation.

The reading standard (3.1) incorporates these literacy components throughout the grades and takes into consideration individual learning differences and student motivation. Specific to reading, speaking, and listening standards are oral language, decoding, comprehension, vocabulary development, and phonemic awareness. Phonemic awareness, a child's ability to hear, identify, and manipulate individual sounds (phonemes) in spoken words, contributes to early, emergent reading development. Since phonemic awareness is mastered by most students prior to the third grade, these skills are included only at the K–2 grade level. With regard to phonics, even though there are different approaches to teaching phonics, research findings indicate that comprehensive phonics programs should incorporate explicit and systematic phonics instruction. Phonics programs should provide ample opportunities for children to apply what they are learning about letters and sounds to the reading of words, sentences, and stories. Effective instruction in the early grades includes providing students with a variety of literary genres, including decodable books that contain specific letter-sound words they are learning. Hence, students understand that there is a predictable relationship between sounds and letters in spoken and written language, and in the language found in their favorite books.

The expectation for reading at all grade levels is that students will read widely. It is important for all students, including students with disabilities and second language learners, to have multiple opportunities to participate in read-alouds, shared and individual reading of high quality materials. Guided repeated oral reading is an effective way of helping students improve their comprehension and fluency skills. Many studies have found that students who become fluent readers read a great deal (National Reading Panel, 2000). Good readers read and comprehend text using similar strategies. Effective strategies used by successful readers at all grade levels include:

• Drawing from prior knowledge to make meaning from print;
• Creating visual images in one's mind to enhance understanding;
• Monitoring one's own reading and checking for understanding;
• Asking questions to identify key points in text and remembering them;
• Making conscious inferences about important information presented;
• Synthesizing new information with existing understanding about a topic;
• Summarizing and understanding how different parts of text are related; and
• Evaluating and forming opinions about ideas presented.

In the language arts classroom, the role of writing is an integral part of reading instruction and offers a means for readers to extend and clarify their ideas. Students need many opportunities to write each day. Through writing workshops, students learn specific writing strategies and produce their own authentic writings. It is important that students at all grade levels write a range of pieces, including narrative, persuasive, informational, fiction, and poetry. In addition, there should be a seamless integration of word processing activities into a program of reading and writing instruction. Technology can be used as an effective tool for literacy tasks, and can facilitate reading comprehension and provide individualized instruction in areas like vocabulary development, phonemic awareness, and word processing.

Standards and Strands

There are five language arts literacy standards, each of which has lettered strands and learning expectations for individual grades (K–4) and small grade-level clusters (5–6, 7–8, 9–12). The standards and strands are outlined below:

3.1 Reading

A. Concepts About Print
B. Phonological Awareness
C. Decoding and Word Recognition
D. Fluency
E. Reading Strategies (before, during, and after reading)
F. Vocabulary and Concept Development
G. Comprehension Skills and Response to Text
H. Inquiry and Research

3.2 Writing

A. Writing as a Process
B. Writing as a Product
C. Mechanics, Spelling, and Handwriting
D. Writing Forms, Audiences, and Purposes

3.3 Speaking

A. Discussion
B. Questioning (Inquiry) and Contributing
C. Word Choice
D. Oral Presentation

3.4 Listening

A. Active Listening
B. Listening Comprehension

3.5 Viewing and Media Literacy

A. Constructing Meaning
B. Visual and Verbal Messages
C. Living with Media

Executive Order No. 8 on Literacy Standards Task Force (February 25, 2002) requires the Department of Education to develop literacy standards in grades 2, 3, and 4. This mandate supports the development of individual grade-level indicators in kindergarten through fourth grade for all five language arts, in order to close the literacy achievement gap for all New Jersey students and address the federal requirement for testing in grades 3–8. The new third grade assessment, as well as future state-selected tests, will be aligned with the revised language arts literacy standards.

The early elementary school experiences are critical to school success. Five-year-olds enter school with a wide range of abilities, motivation to learn, and preschool and home literacy experiences. It is understood that some schools continue to provide half-day kindergartens, while others provide full-day programs for children. Half-day kindergarten programs should make every effort to address the prescribed grade-level expectations outlined in this document. It may be necessary for administrators to review their existing kindergarten schedule, program, staff needs, or classroom materials in order for all students to achieve these standards.

Summary

The revised standards for language arts literacy, along with the vision statement, offer a framework for classroom instruction and curriculum development in our schools. While this is a powerful challenge to students, teachers, principals, and parents, it can be met through a united commitment. The singular goal of increasing student achievement through effective instruction in the skills required to live and work in a 21st century global community is the driving force of this challenge and these standards. The primary grades are building blocks that lay the foundation for learning and skill development so that each succeeding grade builds on the foundation achieved by all students in their efforts to become fluent readers, writers, speakers, listeners, and viewers. As language arts skills spiral and become increasingly sophisticated, students progress through the grades with increased confidence and proficiency in oral and written language, comprehension, and critical thinking skills. Language skills are essential to furthering learning, communication, career development, and the human spirit.

References

The language arts literacy committee would like to thank and acknowledge the following states for providing standards documents to assist in our standards revisions:

Massachusetts English Language Arts Curriculum Framework: Prepublication Draft, November 2000.

California English Language Arts Content Standards for Public Schools. California Department of Education, 1998.

Texas Language Arts Standards. Texas Department of Education, 1998.

Maryland Reading Standards, and *Standards for Instructional Content in English Language Arts, K–12, July 1999*. Maryland State Department of Education

Pennsylvania Academic Standards for Reading, Writing, Speaking, and Listening. Pennsylvania Department of Education, 1999.

Other References

Calkins, L. (2001). *The Art of Teaching Reading*. New York: Addison-Wesley Educational Publishers, Inc.

Directory of Test Specifications in Language Arts Literacy. New Jersey Department of Education, February 1998.

Griffin, P., Smith, P., & Burrill, L. (1995). *The American Literacy Profile Scales: A Framework for Authentic Assessment*. Portsmouth, NH: Heinemann.

Keene, E. & Zimmerman, S. (1997). *Mosaic of Thought: Teaching Comprehension in a Reader's Workshop*. Heineman Books.

National Reading Panel (2000) *Report of the National Reading Panel: Teaching Children to Read. Reports of the Subgroup.* Washington, DC: National Institute of Child Health and Human Development.

New Standards Performance Standards, English Language Arts. National Center on Education and the Economy and the University of Pittsburgh, 1997.

Ray, Katie Wood (1999). *Wondrous Words: Writers and Writing in the Elementary Classroom.* National Council of Teachers of English.

Reutzel, D. & Cooter, R. (2000). *Teaching Children to Read: Putting the Pieces Together.* Third Edition. Saddle River, NJ: Prentice-Hall, Inc.

Snow, C.E., Burns, S.M., & Griffin, P. (1998). *Preventing Reading Difficulties in Young Children.* Washington, DC: National Academy Press.

Standards for the English Language Arts. National Council of Teachers of English and International Reading Association, 1996.

STANDARD 3.1 (READING)
ALL STUDENTS WILL UNDERSTAND AND APPLY THE KNOWLEDGE OF SOUNDS, LETTERS, AND WORDS IN WRITTEN ENGLISH TO BECOME INDEPENDENT AND FLUENT READERS AND WILL READ A VARIETY OF MATERIALS AND TEXTS WITH FLUENCY AND COMPREHENSION.

Building upon knowledge and skills gained in preceding grades, by the end of grade 12, students will:

A. Concepts About Print/Text

3.1.12.A.1 Interpret and use common textual features (e.g., paragraphs, topic sentence, index, glossary, table of contents) and graphic features, (e.g., charts, maps, diagrams) to comprehend information.

3.1.12.A.2 Identify interrelationships between and among ideas and concepts within a text, such as cause-and-effect relationships.

B. Phonological Awareness

No additional indicators at this grade level

C. Decoding and Word Recognition

3.1.12.C.1 Decode new words using structural and context analysis.

D. Fluency

3.1.12.D.1 Read developmentally appropriate materials (at an independent level) with accuracy and speed.

3.1.12.D.2 Use appropriate rhythm, flow, meter, and pronunciation when reading.

3.1.12.D.3 Read a variety of genres and types of text with fluency and comprehension.

E. Reading Strategies (before, during, and after reading)

3.1.12.E.1 Assess, and apply reading strategies that are effective for a variety of texts (e.g., previewing, generating questions, visualizing, monitoring, summarizing, evaluating).

3.1.12.E.2 Use a variety of graphic organizers with various text types for memory retention and monitoring comprehension.

3.1.12.E.3 Analyze the ways in which a text's organizational structure supports or confounds its meaning or purpose.

F. Vocabulary and Concept Development

3.1.12.F.1 Use knowledge of word origins and word relationships, as well as historical and literary context clues, to determine the meanings of specialized vocabulary.

3.1.12.F.2 Use knowledge of root words to understand new words.

3.1.12.F.3 Apply reading vocabulary in different content areas.

3.1.12.F.4 Clarify pronunciation, meanings, alternate word choice, parts of speech, and etymology of words using the dictionary, thesaurus, glossary, and technology resources.

3.1.12.F.5 Define words, including nuances in meanings, using context such as definition, example, restatement, or contrast.

G. Comprehension Skills and Response to Text

Literary Text

3.1.12.G.1 Apply a theory of literary criticism to a particular literary work.

3.1.12.G.2 Analyze how our literary heritage is marked by distinct literary movements and is part of a global literary tradition.

3.1.12.G.3 Compare and evaluate the relationship between past literary traditions and contemporary writing.

3.1.12.G.4 Analyze how works of a given period reflect historical and social events and conditions.

3.1.12.G.5 Recognize literary concepts, such as rhetorical device, logical fallacy, and jargon, and their effect on meaning.

3.1.12.G.6 Interpret how literary devices affect reading emotions and understanding.

3.1.12.G.7 Analyze and evaluate figurative language within a text (e.g., irony, paradox, metaphor, simile, personification).

3.1.12.G.8 Recognize the use or abuse of ambiguity, contradiction, paradox, irony, incongruities, overstatement, and understatement in text and explain their effect on the reader.

3.1.12.G.9 Analyze how an author's use of words creates tone and mood, and how choice of words advances the theme or purpose of the work.

3.1.12.G.10 Identify and understand the author's use of idioms, analogies, metaphors, and similes, as well as metrics, rhyme scheme, rhythm, and alliteration in prose and poetry.

3.1.12.G.11 Identify the structures in drama, identifying how the elements of dramatic literature (e.g., dramatic irony, soliloquy, stage direction, and dialogue) articulate a playwright's vision.

3.1.12.G.12 Analyze the elements of setting and characterization to construct meaning of how characters influence the progression of the plot and resolution of the conflict.

3.1.12.G.13 Analyze moral dilemmas in works of literature, as revealed by characters' motivation and behavior.

3.1.12.G.14 Identify and analyze recurring themes across literary works and the ways in which these themes and ideas are developed.

Informational Text

3.1.12.G.15 Identify, describe, evaluate, and synthesize the central ideas in informational texts.

3.1.12.G.16 Distinguish between essential and nonessential information.

3.1.12.G.17 Analyze the use of credible references.

3.1.12.G.18 Differentiate between fact and opinion by using complete and accurate information, coherent arguments, and points of view.

3.1.12.G.19 Demonstrate familiarity with everyday texts such as job and college applications, W-2 forms, contracts, etc.

3.1.12.G.20 Read, comprehend, and be able to follow information gained from technical and instructional manuals (e.g., how-to books, computer manuals, instructional manuals).

3.1.12.G.21 Distinguish between a summary and a critique.

3.1.12.G.22 Summarize informational and technical texts and explain the visual components that support them.

3.1.12.G.23 Evaluate informational and technical texts for clarity, simplicity, and coherence and for the appropriateness of graphic and visual appeal.

3.1.12.G.24 Identify false premises in an argument.

3.1.12.G.25 Analyze foundational U.S. documents for their historical and literary significance and how they reflect a common and shared American Culture (e.g., The Declaration of Independence, The Preamble of the U.S. Constitution, Abraham Lincoln's "Gettysburg Address," Martin Luther King's "Letter from Birmingham Jail").

H. Inquiry and Research

3.1.12.H.1 Select appropriate electronic media for research and evaluate the quality of the information received.

3.1.12.H.2 Develop materials for a portfolio that reflect a specific career choice.

3.1.12.H.3 Develop increased ability to critically select works to support a research topic.

3.1.12.H.4 Read and critically analyze a variety of works, including books and other print materials (e.g., periodicals, journals, manuals), about one issue or topic, or books by a single author or in one genre, and produce evidence of reading.

3.1.12.H.5 Apply information gained from several sources or books on a single topic or by a single author to foster an argument, draw conclusions, or advance a position.

3.1.12.H.6 Critique the validity and logic of arguments advanced in public documents, their appeal to various audiences, and the extent to which they anticipate and address reader concerns.

3.1 12.H.7 Produce written and oral work that demonstrates synthesis of multiple informational and technical sources.

3.1.12.H.8 Produce written and oral work that demonstrates drawing conclusions based on evidence from informational and technical text.

3.1.12.H.9 Read and compare at least two works, including books, related to the same genre, topic, or subject and produce evidence of reading (e.g., compare central ideas, characters, themes, plots, settings) to determine how authors reach similar or different conclusions.

STANDARD 3.2 (WRITING)
ALL STUDENTS WILL WRITE IN CLEAR, CONCISE, ORGANIZED LANGUAGE THAT VARIES IN CONTENT AND FORM FOR DIFFERENT AUDIENCES AND PURPOSES.

Building upon knowledge and skills gained in preceding grades, by the end of grade 12, students will:

A. Writing as a Process (prewriting, drafting, revising, editing, postwriting)

3.2.12.A.1 Engage in the full writing process by writing daily and for sustained amounts of time.

3.2.12.A.2 Define and narrow a problem or research topic.

3.2.12.A.3 Use strategies such as graphic organizers and outlines to plan and write drafts according to the intended message, audience, and purpose for writing.

3.2.12.A.4 Analyze and revise writing to improve style, focus and organization, coherence, clarity of thought, sophisticated word choice and sentence variety, and subtlety of meaning.

3.2.12.A.5 Exclude extraneous details, repetitious ideas, and inconsistencies to improve writing.

3.2.12.A.6 Review and edit work for spelling, usage, clarity, and fluency.

3.2.12.A.7 Use the computer and word-processing software to compose, revise, edit, and publish a piece.

3.2.12.A.8 Use a scoring rubric to evaluate and improve own writing and the writing of others.

3.2.12.A.9 Reflect on own writing and establish goals for growth and improvement.

B. Writing as a Product (resulting in a formal product or publication)

3.2.12.B.1 Analyze characteristics, structures, tone, and features of language of selected genres and apply this knowledge to own writing.

3.2.12.B.2 Critique published works for authenticity and credibility.

3.2.12.B.3 Draft a thesis statement and support/defend it through highly developed ideas and content, organization, and paragraph development.

3.2.12.B.4 Write multiparagraph, complex pieces across the curriculum using a variety of strategies to develop a central idea (e.g., cause-effect, problem/solution, hypothesis/results, rhetorical questions, parallelism).

3.2.12.B.5 Write a range of essays and expository pieces across the curriculum, such as persuasive, analytic, critique, or position paper, etc.

3.2.12.B.6 Write a literary research paper that synthesizes and cites data using researched information and technology to support writing.

3.2.12.B.7 Use primary and secondary sources to provide evidence, justification, or to extend a position, and cite sources from books, periodicals, interviews, discourse, electronic sources, etc.

3.2.12.B.8 Foresee readers' needs and develop interest through strategies such as using precise language, specific details, definitions, descriptions, examples, anecdotes, analogies, and humor as well as anticipating and countering concerns and arguments and advancing a position.

3.2.12.B.9 Provide compelling openings and strong closure to written pieces.

3.2.12.B.10 Employ relevant graphics to support a central idea (e.g., charts, graphic organizers, pictures, computer-generated presentation).

3.2.12.B.11 Use the responses of others to review content, organization, and usage for publication.

3.2.12.B.12 Select pieces of writing from a literacy folder for a presentation portfolio that reflects performance in a variety of genres.

3.2.12.B.13 <u>Write sentences of varying length and complexity using precise vocabulary to convey intended meaning.</u>

C. Mechanics, Spelling, and Handwriting

3.2.12.C.1 Use Standard English conventions in all writing (sentence structure, grammar and usage, punctuation, capitalization, spelling).

3.2.12.C.2 Demonstrate a well-developed knowledge of English syntax to express ideas in a lively and effective personal style.

3.2.12.C.3 Use subordination, coordination, apposition, and other devices effectively to indicate relationships between ideas.

3.2.12.C.4 Use transition words to reinforce a logical progression of ideas.

3.2.12.C.5 Use knowledge of Standard English conventions to edit own writing and the writing of others for correctness.

3.2.12.C.6 Use a variety of reference materials, such as a dictionary, grammar reference, and/or internet/software resources to edit written work.

3.2.12.C.7 Create a multipage document using word processing software that demonstrates the ability to format, edit, and print.

D. Writing Forms, Audiences, and Purposes (exploring a variety of forms)

3.2.12.D.1 Employ the most effective writing formats and strategies for the purpose and audience.

3.2.12.D.2 Write a variety of essays (for example, a summary, an explanation, a description, a literary analysis essay) that:

- Develops a thesis;
- Creates an organizing structure appropriate to purpose, audience and context;
- Includes relevant information and excludes extraneous information;
- Makes valid inferences;
- Supports judgments with relevant and substantial evidence and well-chosen details; and
- provides a coherent conclusion.

3.2.12.D.3 Evaluate the impact of an author's decisions regarding tone, word choice, style, content, point of view, literary elements, and literary merit, and produce an interpretation of overall effectiveness.

3.2.12.D.4 Apply all copyright laws to information used in written work.

3.2.12.D.5 When writing, employ structures to support the reader, such as transition words, chronology, hierarchy or sequence, and forms, such as headings and subtitles.

3.2.12.D.6 Compile and synthesize information for everyday and workplace purposes, such as job applications, resumes, business letters, college applications, and written proposals.

3.2.12.D.7 Demonstrate personal style and voice effectively to support the purpose and engage the audience of a piece of writing.

3.2.12.D.8 Analyze deductive arguments (if the premises are all true and the argument's form is valid, the conclusion is true) and inductive arguments (the conclusion provides the best or most probable explanation of the truth of the premises, but is not necessarily true).

STANDARD 3.3 (SPEAKING)
ALL STUDENTS WILL SPEAK IN CLEAR, CONCISE, ORGANIZED LANGUAGE THAT VARIES IN CONTENT AND FORM FOR DIFFERENT AUDIENCES AND PURPOSES.

Building upon knowledge and skills gained in preceding grades, by the end of grade 12, students will:

A. Discussion

3.3.12.A.1 Support a position integrating multiple perspectives.

3.3.12.A.2 Support, modify, or refute a position in small- or large-group discussions.

3.3.12.A.3 Assume leadership roles in student-directed discussions, projects, and forums.

3.3.12.A.4 Summarize and evaluate tentative conclusions and take the initiative in moving discussions to the next stage.

B. Questioning (Inquiry) and Contributing

3.3.12.B.1 Ask prepared and follow-up questions in interviews and other discussions.

3.3.12.B.2 Extend peer contributions by elaboration and illustration.

3.3.12.B.3 Analyze, evaluate, and modify group processes.

3.3.12.B.4 Select and discuss literary passages that reveal character, develop theme, and illustrate literary elements.

3.3.12.B.5 Question critically the position or viewpoint of an author.

3.3.12.B.6 Respond to audience questions by providing clarification, illustration, definition, and elaboration.

3.3.12.B.7 Participate actively in panel discussions, symposiums, and/or business meeting formats (e.g., explore a question and consider perspectives).

3.3.12.B.8 Paraphrase comments presented orally by others to clarify viewpoints.

3.3.12.B.9 Give and follow spoken instructions to perform specific tasks to answer questions or to solve problems.

C. Word Choice

3.3.12.C.1 Select and use precise words to maintain an appropriate tone and clarify ideas in oral and written communications.

3.3.12.C.2 Improve word choice by focusing on rhetorical devices (e.g., puns, parallelism, allusion, alliteration).

D. Oral Presentation

3.3.12.D.1 Speak for a variety of purposes (e.g., persuasion, information, entertainment, literary interpretation, dramatization, and personal expression).

3.3.12.D.2 Use a variety of organizational strategies (e.g., focusing idea, attention getters, clinchers, repetition, and transition words).

3.3.12.D.3 Demonstrate effective delivery strategies (e.g., eye contact, body language, volume, intonation, and articulation) when speaking.

3.3.12.D.4 Edit drafts of speeches independently and in peer discussions.

3.3.12.D.5 Modify oral communications by sensing audience confusion and make impromptu revisions in oral presentation (e.g., summarizing, restating, adding illustrations/details).

3.3.12.D.6 Use a rubric to self-assess and improve oral presentations.

STANDARD 3.4 (LISTENING)
ALL STUDENTS WILL LISTEN ACTIVELY TO INFORMATION FROM A VARIETY OF SOURCES IN A VARIETY OF SITUATIONS.

Building upon knowledge and skills gained in preceding grades, by the end of grade 12, students will:

A. Active Listening

3.4.12.A.1 Discuss, analyze, and extend ideas heard orally.

3.4.12.A.2 Distinguish emotive from persuasive oral rhetoric.

3.4.12.A.3 Demonstrate active listening by taking notes, asking relevant questions, making meaningful comments, and providing constructive feedback to ideas in a persuasive speech, oral interpretation of a literary selection, or scientific or educational presentation.

3.4.12.A.4 Identify and define unfamiliar vocabulary through context in oral communications.

3.4.12.A.5 Analyze how a speaker's word choice and nonverbal cues reveal purpose, attitude, and perspective.

B. Listening Comprehension

3.4.12.B.1 Summarize, make judgments, and evaluate the content and delivery of oral presentations.

3.4.12.B.2 Evaluate the credibility of a speaker.

3.4.12.B.3 Determine when propaganda and argument are used in oral forms.

3.4.12.B.4 Listen and respond appropriately to a debate.

3.4.12.B.5 Follow oral directions to perform specific tasks to answer questions or solve problems.

3.4.12.B.6 Paraphrase information presented orally by others.

3.4.12.B.7 Analyze the ways in which the style and structure of a speech support or confuse its meaning or purpose.

STANDARD 3.5 (VIEWING AND MEDIA LITERACY)
ALL STUDENTS WILL ACCESS, VIEW, EVALUATE, AND RESPOND TO PRINT, NONPRINT, AND ELECTRONIC TEXTS AND RESOURCES.

Building upon knowledge and skills gained in preceding grades, by the end of grade 12, students will:

A. Constructing Meaning from Media

3.5.12.A.1 Understand that messages are representations of social reality and vary by historic time periods and parts of the world.

3.5.12.A.2 Identify and evaluate how a media product expresses the values of the culture that produced it.

3.5.12.A.3 Identify and select media forms appropriate for the viewer's purpose.

3.5.12.A.4 Examine the commonalities and conflicts between the visual and print messages (e.g., humor, irony, or metaphor) and recognize how words, sounds, and images are used to convey the intended messages.

B. Visual and Verbal Messages

3.5.12.B.1 Analyze media for stereotyping (e.g., gender, ethnicity).

3.5.12.B.2 Analyze visual techniques used in a media message for a particular audience and evaluate their effectiveness.

3.5.12.B.3 Analyze the effects of media presentations and the techniques used to create them.

3.5.12.B.4 Compare and contrast how the techniques of three or more media sources affect the message.

C. Living with Media

3.5.12.C.1 Use print and electronic media texts to explore human relationships, new ideas, and aspects of culture (e.g., racial prejudice, dating, marriage, family and social institutions, cf. health and physical education standards and visual and performing arts standards).

3.5.12.C.2 Identify and discuss the political, economic, and social influences on news media.

3.5.12.C.3 Identify and critique the forms, techniques (e.g., propaganda), and technologies used in various media messages and performances.

3.5.12.C.4 Create media presentations and written reports using multimedia resources using effective images, text, graphics, music, and/or sound effects that present a distinctive point of view on a topic.

APPENDIX B: NEW JERSEY REGISTERED HOLISTIC SCORING RUBRIC

In Scoring, consider the grid of written language Score	Inadequate Command 1	Limited Command 2	Partial Command 3	Adequate Command 4	Strong Command 5	Superior Command 6
Content & Organization	• May lack opening and/or closing • Minimal response to topic; uncertain focus • No planning evident; disorganized • Details random, inappropriate, or barely apparent	• May lack opening and/or closing • Attempts to focus • May drift or shift focus • Attempts organization • Few, if any, transitions between ideas • Details lack elaboration, i.e., highlight paper	• May lack opening and/or closing • Usually has single focus • Some lapses or flaws in organization • May lack some transitions between ideas • Repetitious details • Several unelaborated details	• Generally has opening and/or closing • Single focus • Ideas loosely connected • Transition evident • Uneven development of details	• Opening and closing • Single focus • Sense of unity and coherence • Key ideas developed • Logical progression of ideas • Moderately fluent • Attempts compositional risks • Details appropriate and varied	• Opening and closing • Single, distinct focus • Unified and coherent • Well-developed • Logical progression of ideas • Fluent, cohesive • Compositional risks successful • Details effective, vivid, explicit, and/or pertinent
Usage	• No apparent control • Severe/numerous errors	• Numerous errors	• Errors/patterns of errors may be evident	• Some errors that do not interfere with meaning	• Few errors	• Very few, if any, errors
Sentence Construction	• Assortment of incomplete and/or incorrect sentences	• Excessive monotony/same structure • Numerous errors	• Little variety in syntax • Some errors	• Some errors that do not interfere with meaning	• Few errors	• Very few, if any, errors
Mechanics	• Errors so severe they detract from meaning	• Numerous serious errors	• Patterns of errors evident	• No consistent pattern of errors • Some errors that do not interfere with meaning	• Few errors	• Very few, if any, errors

Non-Scorable Responses	NR = No Response	Student wrote too little to allow reliable judgment of his/her writing.
	OT = Off Topic/Off Task	Student did not write on the assigned topic/task, or the student attempted to copy the prompt.
	NE = Not English	Student wrote in a language other than English.
	WF = Wrong Format	Student refused to write on the topic, or the writing task folder was blank.

Content & Organization	Usage	Sentence Construction	Mechanics
• Communicates intended message to intended audience • Relates to topic • Opening and closing • Focused • Logical progression of ideas • Transitions • Appropriate details and information	• Tense formation • Subject-verb agreement • Pronouns usage/agreement • Word choice/meaning • Proper modifiers	• Variety of type, structure, and length • Correct construction	• Spelling • Capitalization • Punctuation

APPENDIX C: LANGUAGE ARTS LITERACY OPEN-ENDED SCORING RUBRIC FOR READING, LISTENING, AND VIEWING

Sample Task: The author takes a strong position on voting rights for young people. Use information from the text to support your response to the following.

*Requirements: Explain the author's position on voting.
Explain how adopting such a position would affect young people like you.

Points	Criteria
4	A 4-point response clearly demonstrates understanding of the task, completes all requirements, and provides an insightful explanation/opinion that links to or extends aspects of the text.
3	A 3-point response demonstrates an understanding of the task, completes all requirements, and provides some explanation/opinion using situations or ideas from the text as support.
2	A 2-point response may address all of the requirements, but demonstrates a partial understanding of the task, and uses text incorrectly or with limited success resulting in an inconsistent or flawed explanation.
1	A 1-point response demonstrates minimal understanding of the task, does not complete the requirements, and provides only a vague reference to or no use of the text.
0	A 0-point response is irrelevant or off-topic.

Requirements for these items will vary according to the task.

APPENDIX D: LANGUAGE ARTS LITERACY NEW JERSEY REVISING/EDITING SCORING GUIDE

Score Point Scale	0	1	2	3	4
Content & Organization • central focus • relevant supporting details • use of transitions and other devices to ensure cohesiveness	no attention to opening or closing; no focus; no organization of ideas	minimal attention to opening or closing; some details but no elaboration; no transitions; unable to focus	limited attention to opening and/or closing; progression of ideas but flawed or uneven; may attempt to use transitions	general attention to opening and closing; sense of focus; some use of transitions, but uneven development may be overlooked	consistent attention to opening and closing; single, distinct focus; organization and elaboration of ideas; logical and cohesive use of transitions
Sentence Construction • subordination/coordination • sentence fragments and run-on sentences • sentence combining • additional words to complete meaning	incomplete/incorrect sentences	some sentence construction but marked by monotony and/or awkward syntax; no sense of rhetorical modes	some control of syntax; simple sentence structure, but little or no variety	control of syntax; eliminates excessive monotony; varied sentence structure	syntactic and rhetorical sophistication; subordination and coordination; avoids wordiness
Usage • verbs (tense/agreement) • pronouns (number/agreement) • parallel structure • correct modifiers	numerous and/or serious errors ignored; inability to apply rules	some errors corrected but generally inconsistent application of rules	inconsistent in correcting errors; knowledge of rules but inability to utilize them effectively or consistently	errors corrected, but some may be overlooked; general knowledge and application of rules	knowledge and application of rules, leaving few, if any, errors
Mechanics • spelling • punctuation • capitalization	numerous and serious errors are ignored; inability to apply rules	inability to apply rules; errors, but inconsistently corrected; may create some errors where none existed	knowledge of rules, but some inconsistency in application; patterns of errors remain	errors, though some may be overlooked; knowledge and application of rules	errors, leaving few, if any; knowledge and application of rules
Word choice	no attention to word choice	limited word choice	relies on familiar vocabulary	varied vocabulary with some use of rich words	consistent use of rich words and images to develop topic